THE RIGHT OF PATRONAGE

ACCORDING TO

THE CODE OF CANON LAW

A DISSERTATION

SUBMITTED TO

THE FACULTY OF CANON LAW OF THE
CATHOLIC UNIVERSITY OF AMERICA

IN PARTIAL FULFILLMENT OF THE REQUIREMENTS
FOR THE DEGREE OF
DOCTOR IN CANON LAW

BY

REV. JOHN A. GODFREY, S. T. B., J. C. L.
PRIEST OF THE ARCHDIOCESE OF PHILADELPHIA

THE CATHOLIC UNIVERSITY OF AMERICA
WASHINGTON, D. C.
1924

NIHIL OBSTAT:
THOMAS JOSEPH SHAHAN, S.T.D.,
Censor Deputatus.

IMPRIMATUR:
M. J. CURLEY, D.D.,
Archiepiscopus Baltimorensis.

4/29/1924.

UNIVERSITAS CATHOLICA AMERICAE
WASHINGTONII

FACULTAS JURIS CANONICI
1923-1924

No. 21

TABLE OF CONTENTS

FOREWORD

It may perhaps surprise the reader to find one writing in this pragmatic age on a subject of little or no practical importance to English-speaking peoples. His surprise will be still greater when he reflects that with the promulgation of the Code of Canon Law it is the mind of the Church to abolish the Right of Patronage.[1] A final reason for wonderment will arise from the fact that among us in America, this canonical right has never existed.[2]

But many reasons have urged the present work, despite these manifest handicaps.

First, there is a dearth of English works on this subject. The publication of the Code affords us occasion in some measure to fill this void.

Secondly, the New Law has introduced many changes into the former canonical discipline. These changes should be known and explained.

Finally, the important role which this canonical institution has played in the history of Canon Law is in itself sufficient justification of our efforts.

Written, moreover, as a dissertation in partial fulfillment of the requirements for the degree of Doctorate in Canon Law, a consideration of the chapter on Patronage in the Code appears an apt one to introduce the student of Canon Law into the whole "ethos" or spirit of the new legislation.

It is common knowledge that the Code of Canon Law introduced many changes into the older canonical discipline. At first sight, these variations appear radical. They seem entirely to uproot the former law, and to set up a new system of laws in its stead. But this is not true, as a worthy non-Catholic canonist amply demonstrates.[3] All in all, the Code brings with it little that is new. It merely draws out of the confused mass of

1 Cf. canon 1450, par. 1.

2 Smith, "Elements of Ecclesiastical Law," I, 168.

3 Stutz, U. 57.

previous church legislation its substance and spirit, formulates anew, when necessary, old laws, and incorporates them into a compact and co-ordinated whole.

Of course, new legislation is not wanting in the Code. This was expected. The decrees of Codification and Promulgation announced that corrections, revisions and supplements would be effected by the rewriting and codification of the Canons.[4] But the vast majority of the changes are only of a lesser nature, a necessary consequence, as it were, of the recasting of that "heap of laws, one piled upon the other,"[5] which composed the older canonical discipline, and a result of the reasonings of the approved authors upon the disputed points into which the changes were made.

What is true of the Code in general in this matter, is verified in particular in the chapter on the Right of Patronage. There are many changes from the old law in the New Legislation concerning patronage;[6] almost one might say, "Tot mutationes quot canones," as many changes as there are canons. But, with perhaps one exception, these changes are not radical. They merely decide questions formerly controverted, or state more forcefully than the older canons the traditional, juridical views of the Church on this canonical institution.

To formulate the new law on patronage, the Legislator has taken the sum total of canons, decrees, decisions and rules, which deal with our subject in the older sources of Canon Law, and has codified their substance and spirit into twenty-four fairly brief canons. Among these sources, there are fifty-four chapters of the old "Corpus Juris Canonici," thirteen of the Council of Trent, and many others from bulls, apostolic constitutions, rules of the Sacred Chancery, etc.

Of the canons dealing expressly with patronage in the "Corpus Juris Canonici," those found in the authentic collections are worthy of note. They are as follows:

4 Stutz, U. 57-63.

5 Preface to *Codex Juris Canonici*, p. XXVII.

6 Cf. canons 1448, 1450, 1451-2-3-6-7, 1471.

Thirty-one from the Decretals of Gregory IX.[7]

One from the Sextus of Boniface VIII.[8]

Two from the Clementinae of Clement V.[9]

Besides these there were several chapters of the Council of Trent dealing with the subject.[10] They, too, were universal and authentic church-law.

The dominant note in the whole chapter on the "Juspatronatus" in the Code is sounded in canon 1450, whereby, as we shall see in our chapter on this canon, the Law-giver wishes to abolish entirely this right in the course of time. We call attention to this because it, too, bears a striking analogy to the spirit of the new law in general, inasmuch as it manifests a refinement and, so to speak, a crystallization, of the old law; with a view to giving a purer conception of the mind of the legislator, and thus to avoid the recurrence of the many wranglings and disputes to which the former law had given rise.

With these considerations before us, we have undertaken the present study.

The dissertation were better called "An Introduction to the Right of Patronage," for in reality, the reader has not been given in these pages more than an introductory treatise of so large a subject. Dozens of books of no mean folio-content have been written in other languages, especially in German and French,[11] on the Juspatronatus. This work, therefore, merely introduces the reader into this almost boundless region, dwelling in particular on the legislation of the Code, and giving only the most general directions which one must follow in view of the new law.

A word as to our method. In the discussion of the canons, it has been thought wise to adopt the form of

7 Cc. 1-31, X, *de jure patronatus*, III, 38.

8 C. un. *de jure patronatus*, III, 19 in VI°.

9 Cc. 1, 2, *de jure patronatus*, III, 12 in Clem.

10 Sess. VII *de ref.* c. 13; Sess. XIV, *de ref.* cc. 12-13; Sess. XXV, *de ref.* c. 9.

11 Cf. Archiv. 85, 489 footnote.

a commentary, adhering as closely as possible to the order of the Code. This method appears at once the more in conformity with the method suggested by the S. Cong. for Universities and Colleges of General Studies,[12] and makes for better and more orderly treatment of our subject.

To obtain a fuller understanding of the meaning of the terms "patron" and "patronage" we prelude a chapter on the origin and meaning of these words in both civil and canon law, and also a chapter on the historical development of the right of patronage. In an appendix, we discuss the traces of the right of patronage in the Church in the United States of America.

In conclusion, we acknowledge with grateful thanks the kind assistance of the reverend Faculty of Canon Law in the Catholic University of America in the preparation of our manuscript. To the Rev. Valentine Schaaf, O.F.M., J.C.D., and to the Rev. Hubert L. Motry, S.T.D., J.C.D., we express special thanks for the correction of the proofs.

12 A. A. S. IX, 439.

CHAPTER I

THE TERMS "PATRON" AND "RIGHT OF PATRONAGE" THEIR ORIGIN AND MEANING

Patron, or "patronus," whence the term "juspatronatus," or right of patronage, is derived from the Latin word "pater"—father.[1] It is the name now given in canon law to the Catholic founder of a church, chapel or benefice, who has obtained, by a concession of the Church, the right to present to the local Ordinary a worthy candidate upon whom he wishes the church or benefice of his foundation to be conferred in case of vacancy, and who besides has the right to certain useful and honorary privileges.[2] The collective right to this sum of privileges, with its duties, is designated the "right of patronage."[3] These are the meaning of the words "patron" and "patronage" or "right of patronage" in the present dissertation.

The terms "patronus" and "juspatronatus" in this sense did not appear in canon law until the latter half of the eighth century,[3a] although the canonical right underlying the terms arose at least three centuries prior to this time.[4] This the texts of the next chapter will show.

The first text in which the word "juspatronatus," in the sense of a founder of a church who enjoyed the right

1 "Ratio est, quia fundans ecclesiam dicitur quasi pater, quia deducit ecclesiam de non esse ad esse, jurta Doctores relatos a Lambertino de Jurepatron. Lib. 1, qu. 1, art. 2, n. 9." *De Fargna* vol. 1, page 5.

2 C. 1448 CIC; cf. *Kirchenlexicon*, vol. 9, v. patron.

3 Cf. Augustine, vol. 6, page 524; The jus patronatus is also called in English, the "right of advowson." The term "advowson" is used chiefly in English law. "Patronage" or "right of patronage" are more precise terms we think, in canon law. Cf. Catholic Encyclopedia, vol. XI, v. "patron and patronage."

3a P. Thomas, p. 107.

4 Kirchenlexicon, vol. 9, v. patron; See also next chapter of this work.

to designate a cleric who should serve the church of his foundation (the substantial part of the right of patronage)[4a] is a text from the archives of the Archbishop of Luçon (Lucensis), in 759. Gregory, son of Maurice, had built upon his own soil a chapel in honor of St. Donatus. In the chart of foundation, he makes over to his church, his whole fortune, house, garden, court-yard, movable and immovable property, etc., reserving to himself, during his lifetime, only the usufruct of his estate, and the *right of patronage,* i.e., the right to govern and direct his foundation and the right to choose the titulary (i.e., rector) of the church.[5] A similar use of the term "jus patronatus" is found in a text from the same archives of the year 765.[6] A third instance is had in the text of a speech of Hincmar, Archbishop of Rheims, in the year 874.[6a] But at this epoch, the terms occur but rarely in this sense.

Not until the thirteenth and fourteenth centuries were the terms in current use.[7] Up to this time the names

4a Wernz II, 401.

5 "Gregorius Mauricii filius se ac sua omnia offert ecclesiae sancti Donati a se aedificatae in loco Asulari Lucensis agri, servato sibi *jure patronatus* et usufructu bonorum—Res meas in integrum sit in potestate suprascriptae ecclesiae, sic tamen ut dum advivere meruero, in mea sit potestate in ipsa ecclesia sacerdotem ordinandum et usufructuandum suprascriptas res et regendum una cum ipso presbitero, quem inibi ordinavero" *Muratori* "Antiquitates"—Milan 1738-1742—vol. 11, p. 1023; cf. P. Thomas, p. 107 and p. 62, footnote 1.

6 *Muratori* "Antiquitates" 11, p. 1024.

6a Gaudentius—"Bibliotheca medii aevi," p. 16.

7 Cf. John "Steiermark" (in P. Thomas, p. 108-109); "jus praesentationis" as synonym of "juspatronatus," Boczek "Codex Moraviae," 11, n. 289 (year 1237), 111, n. 278 (year 1259), — n. 282 (year 1259),—n. 296 (year 1260); jus collationis as synonym of juspatronatus, ibid. — n. 174,"—Nos juspatronatus ac collationis—fratribus et ecclesiae S. Mariae contulimus—" Cf. P. Thomas, p. 109, for other references.

usually employed to designate the later "patronal" relationship were "senior" and "senior saecularis."[8]

Even in these centuries (13th and 14th) the *meaning* of the expressions "patronus" and "juspatronatus" was not clearly distinguished from other similar canonical rights, such as the *"jus petitionis," "jus electionis," "jus collationis," "jus representationis"* and especially *"jus praesentationis"* and *"jus advocatiae."*[9] The Decretals themselves use *patronus* and *advocatus* synonymously.[10]

Nay more, the *terms themselves jus patronatus* and *patronus* were equivocal in canon law. Thus, Bernard of Pavia, a canonist of the fourteenth century, writes: "Sciendum tamen quod nomen patroni, unde dicitur juspatronatus, aequivoce accipitur. Dicitur enim patronus, qui suo clientelo in causa patrocinium prestet, . . . et dicitur patronus, qui servum manumisit, . . . dicitur etiam patronus, quasi leno, quia patronus est turpitudinis (because he conceals the crime of his wife), . . . dicitur etiam patronus ecclesiae vel hospitalis fundator, vel dotator, vel soli prestitor, ut hic dicitur."[11]

8 Capit. Aquisgran. a. 817, C. 10, in Mon. Germ. Histor. Legg. 1, 207; Cons Metense (Metz) a 888, c 2—Labbe & Cossart "Concilia" IX, p. 413; Conc. Meldense (Maux) c. 2—Migne PL. vol. 140, c. 649; Hincmari Cap. Syn. 1, c. 17—Migne PL., vol. 125, c. 778. Cf. Richter, *Lehrbuch* par. 151, n. 51; Cf. Imbart de la Tour. 215-233.

9 As above, note 8.

10 6, 7, 24, 25, X de jure patronatus 111, 38; The right of advocacy properly so-called was the right (i. e.—onerous right) which certain lay persons, usually of noble birth, possessed, in virtue of which they were bound to represent a particular church or monastery, and to defend its rights against force. The advocates were specially bound to represent their clients before the secular courts. They exercised civil jurisdiction in the domain of the church or monastery, and were bound to protect the church with arms in the event of actual assault. Finally, it was their duty to lead men at arms in the name of the church or monastery, and to command them in the time of war. In return for these services the advocates received certain definite revenues from the church or monastery, which could even be demanced, e. g.—by a lien on the church property. Cf. Ferraris 1, v. advocatus ecclesiae; Hefele, Conciliengeschichte 2 ed., vol. 1, page 83. Cf. also C. 1 C. XXXII, qu. 1; Schmalzgrueber 111, 38 de jurep, n. 100.

11 Summa Bernardi Papiensis L. 111, tib. 33, p. 119 seq. Ed. Lespeyres-Ratisbon 1861.

The equivocacy was still present in canon law at the time of De Fargna (circa a. 1717), who says, in the introduction to his commentary on the right of patronage, "First, there is the right of patronage of the Libertines, which proceeds from the manumission of slaves; secondly, there is the right of patronage in regard to advocates, who are called the patrons of judicial causes; thirdly, the right of patronage which is accepted as the right belonging to founders of churches to present the rector."[12]

Pirhing (†1690), who wrote about a little while before De Fargna (a. 1722), speaks in almost the same words as De Fargna of the ambiguity of these words in law.[13]

But manifold as were the uses of the terms *patronus* and *patronatus,* the ideas underlying the various significations of the terms were clearly distinguished by the authors. When they spoke of *patron* or *right of patronage,* they were always careful to note the sense in which they accepted the words in their discussions.[14]

In the course of time the equivocacy of terminology seems to have disappeared. When the later canonists speak of *patrons* and *right of patronage,* they mean the right of patronage in regard to the founders of churches.[15] This has become the unequivocal sense of the terms; the former ambiguity has disappeared.

But the later canonists cause the student just as much anxiety by their ambiguity as to the *definition* of the right of patronage as the older authors did with their manifold terminological distinctions. When they define patronage, they give two definitions, the one "a shorter definition," which is nothing more than a definition of the right of presentation, which the Code clearly distin-

12 De Fargna 1, p. 2.

13 Pirhing 111, 38, sect. 1, 1.

14 Cf. De Fargna & Pirhing as quoted above (notes 12 and 13). Reiffenstuel 111, 38 *de jure patronatus,* n. 2.

15 *Aichner* 301; *D'Annibale*—Summula Theologiae Moralis 111, 23; *Hinschuis* 111, 136; *Saegmueller,* p. 276; Wernz II, 401.

guishes from the right of patronage, the other an adequate definition, or "more strict" definition of what is really a *juspatronatus.*[16]

Before examining these definitions, it may be asked: How did the terms *patronus* and *juspatronus* come to be used in canon law in regard to the founders of churches?[17]

The authors generally do not discuss the question. Pirhing, it is true, indicates the origin of the terms in the first two senses of the word (viz., as applied to the Libertines and to the advocates of judicial causes), as the "Jus Civile," i. e., the Roman Law.[18] But does the use of the terms *patronus* and *patronatus* in the third sense, that is, as applied to the founders of churches, trace its origin to the Roman Law? Did the canon law borrow these terms, as applied to founders, from Roman Law? The canonists are silent.

Phillimore, the Anglican canonist, seems to be near the truth when he says: "The title of *patron* has arisen from some unexplained confusion respecting the old Roman law terms *patronus* and *advocatus*."[19] One might go farther than Phillimore and trace the term to the analogy of the *whole* patronal legislation of the Roman Law—not merely of the right of advocacy—with the patronal legislation of the canon law. And an explanation of the "unexplained" may be sought in custom. The canonists from the eighth century onwards used the term "juspatronatus" in regard to founders: it is probable that it became the prevailing method of designating the right, for the law of the Decretals sanctioned it.

16 D'Annibale—Summa Theologiae Moralis 111, 23; Saegmueller, p. 276; Wernz II, 401.

17 "Il est assez difficile to preciser le sens et de fixer l'origine des mots *patronus*, *patronatus*, says P. Thomas, p. 107; it is for this reason that we have ventured an explanation.

18 Pirhing 111, 38, sect. I, I.

19 "The Book of Church Law," Blunt-Phillimore—London, 1921, p. 227, footnote.

It is very probable, therefore, that the canon law borrowed its nomenclature in this instance from the Roman law, for there are marked resemblances—if also substantial differences—between patronage in both laws.

To bring out these similarities, it will be necessary to say a few words about persons in Roman law.[20]

In ancient times, the only citizens proper in the Roman Empire were the members of the patrician and gentile families. They alone could participate in the solemnities of the national religion, take part in the government and defense of the state, contract quiritarian (i. e., legal) marriage, hold property, and enjoy the protection of the laws. But alongside of them was a gradually increasing non-citizen population, composed partly of slaves, partly of free-men, which latter class, however, was not admitted to burgess rights. To this class belonged the clients, individuals who had attached themselves in a position of dependence to the heads of patrician houses as their "patrons," in order thereby to secure attachment to a *gens* which would involve *de facto* freedom.

The patrons, according to Roman Law, were obliged to provide their clients with the necessaries of life, and it was the practice of many patrons to make their clients a small grant of land to cultivate to their own advantage. Also, the patron must be the legal advisor of his clients, and must represent them in transactions with third parties, in which the clients, because non-citizens, could not lawfully act. Finally, the patron must be the clients' substitute in litigations.

Clients, in return for this protection, must render their patrons obedience and respect, and, if necessary, pecuniary assistance. Furthermore, they had to support their patrons should the patrons become reduced to penury.

In later Roman law, the legal relations between patrons and clients were somewhat altered, but the basic

20 Cf. Sohm 164-178; Morey, p. 229-238.

relationship remained the same—the patron was a protector, with certain rights and duties, the client, the one protected, or protégé, who also had definite rights and duties.[21]

If we understand *patron* as the founder of a church or benefice, and *client* as the founded church or benefice, the analogy of patronage in both laws is evident. But it is only an analogy, merely an ideological similarity; juridically they are entirely distinct. But the similarities would be sufficient of justify the probability that perhaps *because of them*, the canon law adopted these terms into her legislation.

To return to the general definitions of the Jus patronatus, given by the later canonists. They are the following:

"Est jus seu potestas praesentandi clericum ad beneficium vocans."[22]

"Jus singulare ab ecclesiastica auctoritate ex gratitudine concessum quo certis personis ecclesiasticis sive physicis sive moralibus (patronis) ab ordinariis vel extraordinariis collatoribus hierarchicis distinctis propter causas in jure expressas praerogativae quaedam honorificae et utiles atque opera etiam circa statum officiorum ecclesiasticorum eorumque provisionem et administrationem competunt."[23]

The former of these is Reiffenstuel's definition, and is the one given by practically all the canonists who have written on the subject since the time of the Decretals. But it is a defective definition, or rather, only a partial definition. For one can possess a true *juspatronatus* without possessing the right to present a cleric to the vacancy, e.g.—the right of patronage of a conventual church does not include the right of presentation.[24]

21 Codex Justinianus Lib. 11, tib. VII and VIII.

22 Reiffenstuel 111, 38, de jurepatronatus, n. 3.

23 Wernz II, 401.

24 C. 25, X, de jure patronatus, 111, 38; Wernz II, p. 163, footnote 4.

The latter definition is from Wernz, who styles it, "a more accurate description." It is a good definition, but rather vague. It was, however, the most complete and one of the best definitions found before the Code.

Whatever the ambiguity in the past, the Code settles the question for the future. The *juspatronatus* according to the Code can mean only one thing; it is "A sum of privileges, which together with certain (correlative) duties, are given by a concession of the Church to the Catholic founders of a church, chapel, or benefice, or to those who have a just title from them (the founders)."[25] The *patronus* is the person who possesses this sum of privileges.

25 C. 1448.

CHAPTER II

THE RIGHT OF PATRONAGE
ITS DEFINITION AND DIVISIONS

The Code treats the "juspatronatus," or right of patronage, in Book III, Title XXV, Chapter IV. Title XXV deals with ecclesiastical benefices in general. The chapter on patronage follows immediately upon the chapter which considers the collation of benefices. This order is logical, for the principal mode by which the ordinary "free" collation of benefices is restricted, is by the presentation of a cleric necessarily to be installed in a vacant benefice over which a patron has the right of presentation.[1]

Some canonists think that the treatment of patronage should be included within the third chapter of the title.[2] By this they would indicate that they consider presentation one of the ordinary ways of providing for vacancies in ecclesiastical benefices. The Legislator, by giving the right of patronage a separate chapter, implicitly refutes this view. In another canon of the Code, the view is explicitly rejected: "Ad collationem beneficiorum vacantium, Cardinalis in proprio titulo vel diaconia et Ordinarius loci in proprio territorio habent intentionem in jure fundatam,"[3] that is, the Ordinary of place is ordinarily the one who confers all benefices in his territory; exceptions must be proved.[4]

The positive reasons of the position of the patronal discipline are three—to differentiate the right of patronage from the mere right of presentation, with which many of the older canonists confused it; to remove any mis-

1 Maroto I, 587.

2 E.g. U. Stutz. "Der Geist des Codex" Juris Canonici 47-49.

3 C. 1432, p. 1.

4 Vermeersch II, 763.

conception as to the juridical basis of patronage, which is the *concession of the Church;* finally, a very practical one—to give opportunity for a fuller treatment of the subject than could have been given had it been placed within the former chapter.[5]

The inscription of the chapter in the Code, "De jure patronatus," is the same as that found in the third book of the Decretals of Gregory IX.[6]

The scheme of the new patronal legislation is as follows; it begins with a definition of the "juspatronatus," and gives its necessary and more important divisions. (cc. 1448-1449.) Next comes the most substantial change affected by the new law, a prohibition against setting up new rights of patronage in future. (c. 1450.) The succeeding canon admonishes Ordinaries to persuade patrons to renounce rights of patronage which they now possess, in exchange for spiritual favors. (c. 1451.) Hereupon follow—to the end of the chapter—the laws by which already existing rights of patronage are to be governed. In particular, these canons deal, first, with popular elections and presentations (c. 1452); with the manner in which the right of patronage is transferred to another (c. 1453); with proofs of the right of patronage (c. 1454); with the privileges of patrons (c. 1455); with the right of presentation in general (cc. 1456 to 1465); with with the right of canonical institution (cc. 1466 to 1468); with the duties of patrons (c. 1469); with the extinction of patronage (c. 1470); finally, with the difference between the right of patronage and its principal part, the right of presentation (c. 1471).[7]

5 U. Stutz "Der Geist des Codex" Juris Canonici 47-49.
6 X, *de jure patronatus* III, 38.
7 Cf. Vermeersch II, 775.

PART 1

The Definition of Patronage
Canon 1448

According to the Code, the right of patronage is "a (determinate) sum of privileges, which together with certain duties, are given by the (free) grant of the Church, to Catholic founders of a church, chapel, or benefice, or to those who have a *cause* (i.e., a lawfully recognized title) from them (the founders)."[8]

To define terms is the business of the canonist, not of the legislator. But in this matter, the Legislator makes a condescension, in order to remove the ambiguity which had arisen in the past among those canonists, who defined the juspatronatus merely as the right of presentation.[9]

"In the definition," says Vermeersch, "the Code purposely reminds us that patronage consists not only of privileges, but likewise of duties: whence patrons may be the more easily induced to renounce that onerous right, and not be solicitous about their privileges. It inculcates that the formal origin of the right is to be sought in the concession of the Church, so that it can in no manner be said to be a quasi-native right of the benefactor (i. e., of the patron), as in reality was once contended in Germany. Finally, it places as a necessary condition for the possession of the right the Catholic religion of the founder. It indicates, moreover, that an impelling cause (causa impulsiva) of granting the privilege (i. e., patronage), is the foundation of a church, chapel, or benefice; and it admits that the right can pass to those who, for some reason (i.e., because of some legally recognized title), succeed the founder."[10]

8 "Jus patronatus est summa privilegiorum, cum quibusdam oneribus, quae ex ecclesiae concessione competunt fundatoribus catholicis ecclesiae, capellae aut beneficii, vel etiam eis qui ab illis causam habent." C. 1448.

9 Cc. pp. 7-8 of this work.

10 Vermeersch II, 776.

This quotation from Vermeersch is a good digest of the canon. We shall develop it at some length, discussing the various questions to which his summary gives rise.

To begin with, the doctrine contained in C. 1448 is not new as the note to the canon indicates. It contains substantially the doctrine of the Council of Trent, plus a few opportune changes in words, based on the teaching of the approved doctors, and the decisions of the Congregations and Apostolic Tribunals. Thus the word "Catholic" before "founders," the words "by the free grant of the Church," the word "chapel," were not found expressly in the Tridentine Decree.[11] Neither did the scheme of the Code, which was sent to the Bishops of the world, contain the first and third.[12] But as we shall see, they were the common teaching among the canonists.

The definition applies to all rights of patronage now existing.[13] The Legislator makes no exception. The principle here applies, "Where the law does not distinguish, neither should we distinguish." Wherever, therefore, contrary custom, even sanctioned by the civil law, as in Germany, prevails, and there is a question whether this or that right is to be understood as the right of patronage, we are to apply the principles of the definition here laid down. By their difformity, the custom is to be judged by canons 5 and 30, dealing with custom. (Incidentally, canon 5 deals with customs that have arisen before the Code, canon 30, with those arising after the Code.) As we shall have occasion to speak later on in this chapter of how patronage does and does not arise, we need not develop this point here.

11 Sess. XXV *de ref.* c. 9.

12 Lib. III, can. 626: "Juspatronatus est summa privilegiorum, cum quibusdam oneribus, quae ex ecclesiae concessione competunt fundatoribus ecclesiarum aut beneficiorum vel eitam eis qui ab illis causam habuerunt."

13 S. Cong. Conc. 12 Nov. and 21 and 10 Jun., 1922, A. A. S. XIV, 466.

Now to an exegesis of the canon.

"A sum of privileges." The right of patronage consists not merely of one privilege, as many of the older canonists thought,[14] but rather with the more recent doctors, it comprises a threefold privilege.[15] This threefold privilege is found in canon 1455, viz.: 1—the right of presentation; 2—the right to sustenance in case of need; 3—the right to certain honors. Of these more in a later chapter.

"Together with certain duties." Blat sees in the use of this dependent phrase an indication by the Legislator that the duties of patrons are "rather light," and, so to say, "negative."[16] With a few exceptions, this statement is true. In most cases, the duties, e.g.—building and repairing the churches, etc., of their foundation, are now to a great extent performed by others than themselves.[17] And in cases where the patrons feel that their duties outweigh their privileges, they may freely make use of, and it is the wish of the Lawgiver, that they do, the right to renounce their patronage, according to canon 1451. If, however, patrons will retain their privilege of patronage, their duties likewise remain.[18]

"From the concession of the Church." As will be noticed in a succeeding chapter,[19] this principle, which follows from the divine foundation and constitution of the Church, has been the occasion of much dispute between the Church and civil rulers. The words authoritatively state the juridical basis of the juspatronatus, the "without which not" of the acquisition of this right. Against canonists and civil jurists, the doctors steadily maintained this doctrine. Thus Saegmueller, before the

14 De Fargna I, 2; Pirhing III, 38, sect. 1, I, Reiffenstuel III, 38, *de jurepatronatus*, n. 3; Schmalzgrueber III, 38, *de jurepatronatus*, n. 3.

15 D'Annibale "Summa Theologiae Moralis" III, 23; Aichner, p. 89; Saegmueller 276; Wernz II, 401.

16 Blat III, 351.

17 Cf. c. 1186, n. 2.

18 C. 1451, par. 2.

19 Chapter 3 of this work.

Code, says:[20] "The basis of this right is the concession of the Church, which, however, enters from law, or is presumed, as soon as the conditions prescribed by the law are present." And Pruemmer, after the Code: "The right of patronage is acquired *solely* by the grant of the Church."[21] This was the implicit teaching of the Council of Trent,[22] and of the canonists generally.[23]

In this connection, one cannot deny that other so-called "causae impulsivae" induced the Church to make this concession. Thus, for example, her traditional gratitude towards the benefactors, her desire so to induce the faithful to build churches, and a certain vindication of the claims of the civilly recognized ownership of church property. But the fundamental basis of patronage was the free grant of the Church—necessarily, indeed, in view of her constitutional rights.[24]

"Founders." By this word is understood not only those who have given the soil (fundus), upon which to erect the church, chapel, or benefice, but likewise those who have endowed the same with sufficient resources for their upkeep, and also those who have actually constructed, or been the efficient cause of, the construction of a church, chapel or benefice.[25] The first two are foundation in the strict sense, the latter two, foundation in the wider sense.

In the pre-Code law, if the same person fulfilled all three requirements, viz.—fundatio, dotatio et constructio, he became ipso jure patron, unless he waived his right.[26] When the saying of the Gloss; "Patronum faciunt dos, aedificatio, fundus."[27] Different persons per-

20 Saegmueller, 276-277.

21 Pruemmer, "Manuale," 505.

22 Sess. XXV *de ref.* c. 25.

23 Schmalzgrueber III, 38, de jurepatronatus 2-5; De Fargna I, 2-5; Aichner, p. 89; Saegmueller 275-276; Wernz II, 401.

24 De Fargna I, 2-5; Wernz II, 403-405.

25 Wernz 413-414.

26 Wernz II, 413-414; Saegmueller 280.

27 Gloss to c. 26, C. XVI, qu. 7.

forming conjointly these three acts became co-patrons. And it was an accepted view among the doctors that one who performed any one of the three acts, the other conditions being fulfilled in any manner whatsoever, became a patron.[28] This view was supported by sound reasonings, founded as it was on the law of the Decretals and the Council of Trent.[29] Thus concerning construction, or building (aedificatio)—"To your question, we give the response, that if anyone, with the consent of the Diocesan (i.e., Bishop of the place) has built a church, he thereby acquires the right of patronage."[29a] Concerning endowment, from the Council of Trent, we have the following: "None, moreover, of whatsoever ecclesiastical or secular dignity, can, or ought, obtain, or acquire a right of patronage for any other reason whatsoever, but that he has founded and built anew, a church, chapel, or benefice, or that he has completely endowed, out of his own and proper patrimonial resources, one already erected, which, however, is without sufficient endowment."[30] "Although," says Blat,[31] "it may seem, from the use of the conjunction 'et' between fundaverit and construxerit, of the chapter quoted, that the foundation, i.e.—the giving of the fundus on which to build, without the actual construction, is not sufficient, nevertheless, the particle is to be taken in the disjunctive sense of 'or,' as in many other of the sacred canons (of the Council)." In the above quotation of Gregory IX's Decretal that construction of itself was sufficient.[32] This prescription of the Decretal law was not revoked by the Tridentine law. For another canon of Trent supports this contention, which says: "The S. Synod decrees that the right of patronage is from foundation *or* endowment." [33]

28 Wernz II, 414; Saegmueller 280.

29 C. 2 de *jure patronatus* III, 12 inclem.; Trent, Sess. XIV *de ref.*, c. 12; Sess. XXV *de ref.*, c. 9.

29a C. 25 X, *de jure patronatus* III, 38.

30 Sess. XIV *de ref.*, C. 12—*Waterworth's* translation.

31 Blat III, 353.

32 C. 25 X *de jurepatronatus* III, 38.

33 Sess. XXV *de. ref.*, C. 9.

This theory is of importance to us only in so far as it enables one to judge concerning patronages already existing; new rights of patronage cannot be thus acquired.[34]

"Catholic" founders. The word "catholic" was not in the original scheme of the Code. Its addition is explained by the fact that the exercise of the right of patronage entails some spiritual power, which cannot be lawfully exercised by non-Catholics.[35] Furthermore, it denotes a restriction of the older discipline. According to the canonists before the Code, "Every baptized person was capable of acquiring an ecclesiastical right, who was not prohibited for some special reason of ecclesiastical law." Thus laymen, women and children with the use of reason, could obtain this right.[36] Those who had not yet attained the age of puberty and even illegitimates, could obtain it.[37] But infidels (i.e.—those not baptized) could not obtain this right.[38] Finally apostates, heretics, schismatics, excommunicated and infamous persons could not acquire the juspatronatus.[39] There is a further restriction by the new legislation, now only those rights of patronage, residing in *catholics* are to be recognized.

"Of a *church, chapel or benefice.*" This phrase indicates the object of the right of patronage. Every right of patronage, even as every right in general, postulates a subject, in which a right inheres, an object to which the right is attached, and a juridical fact upon which the right is based. Of the subject of the right of patronage, we shall have occasion to speak when we consider canon 1453. Of the juridical fact on which patronage is based, we have already spoken in our remarks on the word "founders." We speak here of the object to which the right of patronage is attached.

34 C. 1450, par. 1.

35 Schmalzgrueber 1, 38, *de jurepatronatus* nn. 2-5; can. 2263.

36 Wernz II, 409.

37 C. 25 X *de jurepatronatus* III, 38; Wernz 409.

38 Pirhing III, 38, *de jurepatronatus*, n. 20; S. Cong. Inquis. 31 May, 21, Dec., 1873 (In *Archiv.* 37, 361-365).

39 C. I de rescriptis I, 3 in VI°; R. I. 87 in VI°.

According to the Tridentine legislation, the object of the right of patronage was "every and only an ecclesiastical office"[40] provided the juspatronatus was not expressly withdrawn from certain offices. The right of patronage could not be acquired over a precious pavement, over a cemetery, or sepulchre.[41] Neither were any concessions of the right of patronage granted common law over the election of the Roman Pontiff,[42] or in the creation of Cardinals.[43] There was no justification of the right of patronage over episcopal dignities granted by the law of the Decretals. Only when this privilege was given by Apostolic indult could it be lawfully admitted.[44] In the Tridentine legislation, however, and by Concordats,[45] were granted to the rulers of nations many rights of presentation of Bishops to cathedral churches, but this was not in virtue of common law alone, but common law plus the special grant of the Roman Pontiff.[46] But there was no right of patronage granted to other laymen over cathedral churches, unless this was granted by apostolic indult. Thus the pretension of the lay community of Savoy, February 29, 1744, was rejected.[47] Prelatures and first dignities in cathedral and collegiate chapters, and in conventual churches, were not as a rule subject to the full juspatronatus, i.e., one containing the right of presentation—at least to the lay juspatronatus.[48] Over other offices, such as simple canonries of cathedral churches and of collegiate

40 Sess. XXV *de ref.*, c. 9.

41 Cf. Wernz II, 410.

42 Hefele—"Conciliengeschichte" III, 713.

43 The practice of certain governments of recommending Bishops for the Cardinalate was not based on the juspatronatus. Cf. Wernz II, 410 and footnote 38.

44 X *de electione* I, 6; c. 25 X *de jurepatronatus* III, 38; Giobbio "Lezzioni di diplomatica ecclesiastica" II, 110-125.

45 Sess. XXV *de ref.*, c. 9; *Nussi* 34, 44, 46.

46 Wernz II, 410.

47 Conc. Trid. ed *Richter* 450, n. 2.

48 C. 25 X *de jurepatronatus* III, 38; Wernz II, 410.

churches, theological and penitential prebends not excepted,[49] likewise over parochial churches and other curate and simple benefices, the juspatronatus, with the right of presentation, could be obtained. Over these both the ecclesiastical and lay right of patronage could be acquired.[50]

Over other ecclesiastical offices, which were not benefices, such as the office of Vicar General, rural Deans, judges of the episcopal courts, Defender of the bond of matrimony and ordination, the juspatronatus did not as a rule obtain.[51]

The New Law explicitly mentions churches, chapels, and benefices. If, therefore, the right of patronage is claimed over any office not comprehended under these headings, the presumption of the law is against it, and the right of patronage must be supported by more cogent proofs than would otherwise be demanded by canon 1454.

In this connection, it may be noted that in missionary countries, where ecclesiastical benefices in the strict sense do not exist, and great liberty is necessary in the appointment of rectors, etc., the right of patronage is ordinarily not admitted.[52] "Thus the first provincial Council of Baltimore, optimo jure, declared: No right of patronage of any kind, which the sacred canons recognize, belongs at this time (a. 1829) to any lay congregation, to any body of trustees, or to any other persons whatsoever, in this province."[53] Rights of patronage in such countries must, therefore, be supported by very strict proofs.

"Or to those who have a cause from them." The "or" is to be understood in the conjunctive sense of "and."[54]

49 Cf. S. Cong. Conc. in A. S. S. IV, 177, 353.

50 Conc. Trid. Sess. XXV de ref., c. 9; Lingen & Reuss "Causae Selectae S. Cong. Conc." 256.

51 Wernz II, 410.

52 Wernz II, 411—Wherefore, there are very few cases concerning the juspatronatus in the collection of the Propagation of the Faith.

53 Acta et Decreta Conc. Balt. Plen II. II, 184.

54 Blat III, 353.

"Habere causam" in this connection is equivalent in English to, "to have a lawfully recognized title"; in German, "einen rechtlichen Erwerbsgrund haben."[55]

Thus the Code admits the lawfulness of those patronages which have been acquired by a so-called "derivative" title. In other words, it admits a justification of those patronal rights which are based upon any of the following titles: 1, hereditary or legatine succession; 2, donation; 3, exchange; 4, purchase or sale. This in conformity with the verse of the Gloss:

"Jus patronatus transire facit novus heres,
Res permutata, donatio, venditioque."

For a fuller explanation of these titles, the reader is referred to the chapter dealing with the derogation of the right of patronage.

Before concluding this chapter, there is a question which calls for a discussion which will aid us to a better understanding of the canons which succeed.

The question to which we refer is: Is the juspatronatus a right strictly so called, or is it merely a privilege? If the former, what kind of right is it, especially as regards its extension and its stability?

Canonists give many kinds of rights in their enumerations. According to their scope, or extension, rights are either universal (common, general) or particular (special, singular).

A universal right is one that has force in the whole territory of the Church, or in the whole of the Christian world. A particular right is one whose force extends only to a certain determined and limited part of the world.

A general right is one that has reference to *all* the faithful, a special right, one that refers to a certain class, or a certain body of the faithful.

55 Pruemmer, "Manuale," p. 505, footnote.

A common right is one that constitutes the rule ordinarily to be followed; a jus singulare, or singular right, one that constitutes an exception to the general law, whether favorable or unfavorable; if the exception be favorable, it is called a privilege.

"This meaning of the 'jus singulare,' " says Maroto, "is taken from Roman Law." "A singular right," says Paulus (fr. 16, D. I, 3), "is that which has, against the tenor of law (i.e.—the general rule of law) been introduced on account of some utility by the authority of those constituting it." Concerning this singular right, it is stated in the same place, "but that which has been received contrary to the tenor law, must not be pushed to its consequences." (fr. 14.)

According to their stability, rights are divided into:

1. Jus precarium, or a right of favor.
2. Jus quaesitum, or an acquired right.
3. Jus strictum, or a right simply so called without any qualifying word.

The jus precarium is a right granted by the free will of the legislator. It can be both licitly and validly revoked at the free will of the grantor.

The jus quaesitum is not a right strictly of commutative justice as regards the grantor and its possessor, but only in regard to third persons. It is more firm than the right of favor, but it can be validly revoked by the grantor, e.g., by the Supreme Pontiff. It is founded on a certain agreement between its grantor and its possessor.

The jus strictum, or right simply so called is one due in strict, commutative justice, and inheres so intimately in its possessor that without his consent, it cannot ordinarily be revoked even validly. Sometimes, indeed, it is simply inalienable.

Privileges in Roman Law were understood as certain concessions made by the general laws themselves, but which in one respect had the special signification of a benefit, prerogative, or favor, and in another, had reference to a particular kind of persons, places or things, such were, e.g.—the privileges of restitution in integrum, finding, etc., the privilege of dowry, tax, etc., the privileges of minors, women, soldiers, etc. The laws themselves which granted these benefits were called "privileges," and were distinguished from common law. (fr. 30, 2 D. xxviii, 6; fr. 15, D. xxviii, 6.) They were, therefore, laws pertaining to the jus singulare, whence those laws themselves and the favors granted by them, were also called singular rights.

In Canon Law both classes of privileges exist, but the name and meaning of privilege is adapted chiefly to those favors granted to any particular person, whether physical or moral.

Privileges are granted in Canon Law either "per modum facultatis," which is the ordinary way, or "per modum legis," which is the extraordinary way of granting them.

The Code does not determine explicitly whether the juspatronatus is a right or privilege. It leaves the question to the doctors to decide. Because of the importance of the solution of the question in determining the changes in the new law of patronage, and the consequent vindication of those changes, in particular that of the prohibition of the establishment of future rights of patronage, the present discussion has been introduced.

It would seem that the juspatronatus is singular right, as to its extension, and a jus quaesitum, or acquired right, as to its stability. It is a singular right that enters per modum legis once the conditions required by law (scil. foundation, building, or endowment, with the consent of the Diocesan), have been fulfilled, and that once granted it has the nature of an acquired right, due in strict commutative justice to its possessor as far as third persons are concerned, but at the same time *validly* revocable, even without cause by the Supreme Pontiff.

Thus Ferraris says: "The Pope can, if he wish, freely dispose of patronal benefices, not only ecclesiastical ones, but even those of lay patronage—even though the patrons be unwilling." In this Reiffenstuehl and Fagnanus agree with him. "For since the justapatronatus," he says, "which laymen possess in the Church is gratuitous, and the Church sustains them in its possession by a favor, as is clearly said in the chapter 'Quoniam' (c. 3. X, 111, 38). 'Potestate in qua eos ecclesia hucusque sustinuit, abutuntur.'" From this it is clear that the Pope can in the plenitude of his power derogate such juspatronatus. This according to the first rule of the Sextus: "Omnis res, per quascumque causus nascitur, per easdem dissolvitur."

But, lest the faithful be thereby deterred from the foundation of benefices it is not expedient that the legislator dispose of the right of patronage of the laity, as the doctors commonly teach, and because the Council of Trent says in its 25th Session, Chapter 9, de ref. "It is not *equitable* to take away the rights of patrons, or to violate the pious wills of the faithful in their institutions."

PART 2

Divisions of the Right of Patronage
Canon 1449

The second canon on the juspatronatus, C. 1449, gives the divisions of patronage.

"The Right of Patronage is:

"1. *Real* or *Personal,* according as it attaches to a thing, or directly refers to a person.

"2. *Ecclesiastical, Lay* or *Mixed,* according as the title by which one possesses the right of patronage is ecclesiastical, lay or mixed.

"3. *Hereditary, belonging to a family, belonging to a 'gens'* or *mixed,* according as it passes to heirs, to those who belong to the family or 'gens' of the founder, or to those who are at the same time heirs and belong to the family or 'gens' of the founder."

This canon gives the kinds of patronage which the New Law recognizes. The doctrine is not new, though we should look in vain to find patronages designated in these express terms in the older fonts of law.[1] The terminology is that found commonly among the approved authors, before the Code.[2] Just as the definition of terms pertains rather to the canonists than to the legislator, so too the division of subjects. The divisions proposed are, nevertheless, based upon the sources themselves.[3]

1 Cf. X, *de jure patronatus* III, 38; Conc. Trid. Sess. XXV *de ref.*, c. 9; Sess. XIV *de ref.*, c. 12.

2 Reiffenstuel III, 38, *de jure patronatus* 45-65; Schmalzgrueber III, 38, *de jure patronatus* 6-29; Ferraris V. *juspatronatus* vol. I, 2-18; Wernz II, 401, ad. III.

3 Cf. X *de jure patronatus* III, 38; c. 2 *de jure patronatus* III, 12, in Clem; Conc. Trid. Sess. XXV *de ref.*, c. 9; Sess. XIV *de ref.*, c. 12.

The doctrine of the canon is not proposed "taxative", i.e., in such a manner as to exclude the other divisions found among the doctors.[4] But it does propose the essential divisions of the *juspatronatus*. Other divisions, if we except the so-called juspatronatus regium, (of which in the last chapter), are to be considered accidental to the understanding of the patronal legislation of the new law. Whence, the commentators of the Code omit the older divisions.[5]

The divisions here given regard the so-called *juspatronatus privatum*, in contradistinction to the *juspatronatus regium*, i.e., the patronal rights possessed by private individuals, in opposition to those possessed by rulers.[6] These latter suffer no change, inasmuch as they are usually granted in concordats or by indult, and with these the Code, according to canons 3 and 4, does not deal. Inasmuch, however, as the last canon on patronage, C. 1471, makes an opportune observation concerning the regal juspatronatus, occasion shall be had to say a few words about this canon in the last chapter of our study.

The first number of the canon gives the division of patronage according to the subject in which it inheres, which subject can be either a thing or a person. The second paragraph is according to the title by which a right of patronage is acquired. The third, according to the manner in which a right of patronage can be handed down to others.[7]

In the history of the right of patronage, many kinds of patronage came gradually to be admitted to the founders of churches, chapels, or benefices.[8] Chief

4 The other divisions proposed by the authors before the Code were rather sub-divisions of the three species enumerated in this canon (1449)—cf. Wernz II, 401.

5 Vermeersch II, 778; Blat III, 352.

6 Blat III, 352.

7 Blat III, 352.

8 Phillips VII, 669; Hergenrother-Hollweck 599.

among these varied species were those admitted as a personal privilege to the founders, i. e., granted directly and immediately to a person, not in view of the office or dignity, which he possessed but granted to him or her as a person (ratione sui).[9] Other patronages were attached directly and immediately to the thing (church, chapel, or benefice).[10] The former are known as *personal* rights of patronages, and like personal privileges "follow the person, and are extinguished with him"; the latter are *real* jurapatronatus, and are transmissible to others.

The second number of the canon recalls the motive of gratitude towards benefactors which the Church has steadily manifested in her patronal discipline. As regards the concession of the right of patronage to those benefactors, she has always kept in view the nature (i. e., the juridical nature) of the goods by which the benefactions were made, and granted her rights of patronage accordingly. Thus, if the title, or primary motive, by which one was given a juspatronatus, was purely ecclesiastical, e. g. the office ecclesiastical which one possessed, or foundation of a church, etc., with goods strictly ecclesiastial, his juspatronatus was called an *ecclesiastical* juspatronatus.[11] If one, whether a layman or a cleric, founded a church, etc., out of his own proper patrimonial resources, or out of other private revenue, e.g., out of money left him by a will, etc., he obtained a *lay* right of patronage.[12] If from goods partly lay and partly ecclesiastical, e.g., one-half out of his own private resources, and the other half with goods belonging juridically to the Church, he acquired a *mixed* right of patronage.[13]

Both the real and the personal juspatronatus may be lay, ecclesiastical, or mixed according as the person who

9 C. 10 Council of Orange (a. 441) in c. 1, C. XVI, qu. 5—Labbe & Cossart "Concilia" III, 69; cf. Archiv. 85-492-493.

10 C. 13, X, *de jure patronatus*, III, 38; S. C. Epis. et Reg. 25 Jun., 1850, in Bizzarri, pp. 122-123.

11 C. 6, X, *de off leg.*, I, 30; c. 28, X, *de jure patronatus* III, 38.

12 C. 31, C. XVI, qu. 1; c. 4, C. XVIII, qu. 2.

13 C. 2, *de jure patronatus*, III, 12, in Clem.; cf. Wernz II, 401, ad. III.

exercises it is a layman, or an ecclesiastic, or when it is exercised by a plurality of patrons some of whom are laymen, and others ecclesiastics.[14]

The final division of patronage, in number 3 of the canon is, as has been said, according to the manner in which the right of patronage is handed down or passes on to another.

Hereditary must be understood either as testamentary, natural or legitimate, that is, one belonging to a founder in such manner that he or she may pass it on to another either by will, or by natural succession, or by law. It can be passed on to all the heirs of the founder, either collectively or singly, whether they be natural heirs or heirs according to law, or merely the legatees of a will.[15]

Belonging to a family, or juspatronatus familiare, is that which may be transmitted to those belonging to the family of the founder, whether they be agnati, or cognati.[16] By "agnati" is understood those belonging to the household of the founder. By "cognati" the blood-relatives of the founder.[17]

Belonging to a "gens" or juspatronatus gentilitium, is that which may be handed down to those who belong to the clan of the founder, that is, to those who are "agnati" of the founder, but not blood-relatives.[18] This is De-Luca's opinion[19] at least, in opposition to Blat,[20] who seems to confuse the juspatronatus familiare with the juspatronatus gentilitium.

14 C. 2, *de jure patronatus*, III, 12, in Clem. Wernz II, 401, ad. III.

15 Schmalzgrueber III, 38, *de jure patronatus*, n. 12; Wernz II, 401.

16 Wernz II, 401; D'Annibale "Summa Theologiae Moralis" III, 25, and footnote 23.

17 *Morey* "Outlines of Roman Law," p. 6 and p. 34.

18 D'Annibale "Summa Theologiae Moralis," III, 25, and footnote 23.

19 De Luca—"Diss de jure patronatus," p. 60, 3.

20 Blat III, 352.

A mixed right of patronage is one that can pass only to those who are at the same time members of the family of the founder and likewise members of his clan.[21]

In an hereditary right of patronage, all the heirs are considered of equal rights so far as patronage is concerned.[22]

To determine the species of patronage, it is necessary to examine the bill of foundation, which is, as other privileges, to be interpreted strictly according to its verbal tenor, and is to be neither restricted nor amplified.[23] In view of the new legislation the stricter interpretation is to be given in case of doubt, that is, the interpretation favoring the Church.[24]

21 D'Annibale "Summa" III, 25, and footnote 23; Wernz II, 401.

22 Reiffenstuel III, 38, de jure patronatus, n. 19.

23 Can. 67.

24 Can. 50; "In dubio rescripta quae ad lites referuntur vel—vel denique impetrata fuerunt *ad beneficii ecclesiastici assecutionem*, strictam interpretationem recipiunt ———"

CHAPTER III

The Origin of the Right Itself

The date of origin of the right of patronage is not agreed upon by all canonists. Most catholic canonists[1] together with Dr. Paul Hinschius and Imbart de la Tour, the eminent non-catholic canonists[2] place its origin not later than the fifth century. Kaim[3] sees its beginning much earlier, viz., in the very early days of Christianity, before the recognition of the Christian Religion by the Roman Empire. P. Thomas, a French non-Catholic jurist of some repute, declares for its eleventh century origin.[4]

This divergence of opinion seems to have arisen from two main causes, or rather, from two variations of the same cause. The first of these is the fact that the canonical institution which, in the course of time, became known as the right of patronage, passed through a long period of development; the second, the divers definitions given by the various authors who have written on patronage.

The two principle definitions of patronage as understood by the older canonists, have already been given.

The "Juspatronatus," according to Reiffenstuel, "is the right or power to present a cleric to a vacant ecclesiastical benefice." Or more fully, according to Pirhing, who also gives the shorter definition just given, it is "the honorary, onerous and useful right belonging to

1 *De Fargna* II, p. 2; *Aichner* 89; *Schindler*, in Archio 85-492; *Permaneder*, in "*Kirchenlexicon*" IX, 1620-1621; *Saegmueller* 280-282; Wernz II, 406-408.

2 *Hinschius* II, 619-621; cf. also Imbart de la Tour 117-182.

3 *Kaim, Das Kirchenpatronat nach seiner Entstehung*, etc., Leipzig, 1845.

4 *P. Thomas*, Preface, and pp. 1, 116.

anyone over a church, because with the consent of the Diocesan (Bishop), or ecclesiastical Prelate, he or one from whom he has received a just title, e. g., an heir of the patron, has founded or built or endowed said church." Thus also Fagnanus, De Fargna, Ferraris, Wernz, and a host of others whom these men quote.

The former of these definitions is that of a so-called *incomplete* right of patronage, the latter, that of a *complete* juspatronatus. These are also designated *imperfect* and *perfect* juspatronatus.[5]

If, therefore, the adversaries of the fifth century origin of this right mean that a complete or perfect juspatronatus did not exist at so early a date, there can be no objection to their opinions. If, however, they do not admit that the right of patronage, according to the former definition traces its beginnings back to the fifth century, we cannot share their views. This following discussion will show.

Certain vestiges of what was later to become known as the juspatronatus, or right of patronage, are found in the very early days of the Church.[6] From the very beginning, the Church had always shown herself grateful to benefactors, and had manifested this gratitude by granting them various privileges. St. Chrysostom mentions in one of his sermons that the names of founders of Churches were mentioned in the Holy Sacrifice of the Mass.[7] Likewise, the names of the founders of churches were imposed upon the churches of their foundation (e.g., at Rome, the title of St. Lawrence in Damasus, the title Pamachius, the title St. Lawrence which is called "Lucinae," etc.).[8] Another example is that of the basilica of Constantine, or Lateran. Also, the names were inscribed in the diptychs and were ordered to be read publicly in the churches of foundation.[9]

5 Thomassinus P. II, 1, I c. 29; Philips VI, 21.
6 De Fargna I, p. 2; Saegmueller 275; Wernz II, 406.
7 Homily XVIII in Acta Apostolorum—Ed. Montfacon 9, 151.
8 Wernz II, 406.
9 Wernz II, 406.

But a right of patronage in any adequate sense of the term is not found in those early days. It is generally agreed that during the first four centuries of the Christian Era, there was no necessity for the right of patronage. It was only upon the division of dioceses into parishes, when the faithful began so to increase that the basilica of the Bishops could no longer accommodate them, and upon the foundation of rural parishes to take care of the faithful whom the congestion of the cities forced to the country districts that the right of patronage was introduced. It was granted in order to induce the faithful to build parish churches. (Bingham-Antiquities I, 138-140, 193, 410; Imbart de la Tour, 190-233.)

The first example that a founder received the right to nominate a cleric to the church which he had founded is found in the fifth century, in Gaul.[10] This privilege was there first given to a Bishop who had founded a church in another diocese. The laity did not enjoy this privilege as yet.[11] And even though the right of nomination was given to the Bishop who had founded the Church, the full and unrestricted right of instituting the clerics in the newly founded church resided in the Bishop of the diocese to which the church belonged.[12]

In the Oriental Church at this period was admitted to lay-founders of churches built or endowed by them only a part in the administration of the temporalities of those

10 C. 10 Council of Orange (a 441)—in c. 1, C. 16, qu. 5—Labbe & Cossart "Concilia" III, 69; "Si" quis episcoporum in alienae civitatis territorio ecclesiam aedificare disponit, vel profundi sui negotio aut ecclesiastica utilitate vel pro quacumque sua opportunitate, permissa licentia aedificandi quia prohibere hoc votum nefas est, non praesunat dedicationem, quae illi omnimodis reservatur in cujus territorio ecclesia assurgit, reservato aedificatori episcopo haec gratis ut quos desiderat clericos in re sua videre, ipsos ordinet is cujus territorium est, vel si jam ordinate sunt, ipsos habere acquiescat. Et omnis ecclesiae ipsius gubernatio ad eum in cujus territorio ecclesia surreverit, pertinebit."

11 Imbart de la Tour "Les Paroisses Rurales," 181, footnote, where he refutes the opposite opinion of Hinschius. *Kirchenlexicon* v. Patronatsrecht IX, 1521; *Aichner* 89, n. 2.

12 *Kirchenlexicon*, as in n. 11; Imbart de la Tour 177-182.

churches.[13] Not until the legislation of Justinian (middle of the sixth century), were the lay founders of a church conceded the right to present to the Bishop, by themselves or by their heirs, worthy ecclesiastics, to be instituted in the founded churches.[14] This concession was made in a general manner, but it was a *concession.*

About the same time (middle of the sixth century), or soon after, the right of presentation was conceded to lay-founders in the Western Church.[15] Every right of ownership of a church and its resources ("bono") was, however, expressly refused.[16]

It must here be remarked that in the beginning every right of patronage, cum jure praesentandi (or "seniority," as it was then called,[16a] was only a personal right of the founder.[17] This right was granted "only as long as the founders remained living.[18] It was, therefore, a non-transferable right. Only the right of administration of the goods of the patronal church could be handed down to others.[19]

Thus far, then, in the history of this right, is found only a personal right of patronage, and ownership of

13 I 15 Cod. de ss. eccles. 1, 2.

14 Nov. 57, c. 2; Nov. 123, c. 18; Nov. 123, c. 18; "Si quis oratorii domum aedificaverit et voluent in ea clericos ordinare aut ipse, aut ejus haevedes; si expensas ipsis clericis ministrant, et dignos denominant, denominatos ordinari. Si vero ab eis eliguntur, tanquam indignos prohibent sacrae regulae ordinari, tunc episcopiis quoscumque putaverit meliores, ordinare procuret."

15 C. 31, C. XVI, qu. 1; c. 4, XVIII, qu. 2.

16 Cc. 26, 27, C. XVI, qu. 7.

16a *Senior* was the lord of a manor. Since it was chiefly these feudal lords who were the founders of churches during the middle ages, Senior came to be used as the equivalent of the later term "patronus." The first text in which the term if found in the sense of a founder is in a capitulary of 810, a 3 (apud Boretius, Capitularia regum Francorum, 2 vols. Hanover in Monumenta Germ. historica, p. 178); cf. Imbart de la Tour 215.

17 C. 2, Conc. Tolet. IX, (a 655) in Labbe & Cossart "Concilia" VI, 452.

18 "Quamdiu earundem fundatores ecclesiarum in hoc vita superstites existiterint"—c. 2, Conc. Tolet. IX—Labbe & Cossart VI, 453.

19 C. 31, C. XVI, qu. 7.

churches was not recognized to the founders at this time. Furthermore, these earlier rights of patronage were non-transferable.

The second period in the development of the right of patronage introduces the right of patronage which is found most commonly today, the *real* juspatronatus. This is a transferable and hereditary right, as its history will show.

The "real" right of patronage had its foundation in the law and institutions of the German people.[19a] Among them it was received that a free-born person (ingenuus) to whom belonged the ownership of any fundus (i. e., estate, or land), was likewise owner and native protector of those persons and things which the fundus contained.[20] Whence also churches erected on the fundus were considered part of the ownership, so that they and the clerics serving them were subject to the dominion and protection of the owner. It thus came about that the owner of the church was accustomed to administrate its goods, to institute and invest clerics, in opposition to the principles of canon law, and even to assign the clerics to profane duties. Thus also it came about that churches began to be sold together with the fundus, as things rightfully belonging to the owner,[21] or they were exchanged, handed down as fiefs, or divided among many heirs.[22] And although such churches and oratories very frequently became parochial churches and thence the right of ownership over them ex rei natura ceased, nevertheless, it was the custom among the heirs to retain the right of patronage over them, because they thought that the right of ownership could not thereby be

19a Imbart de la Tour 190-233; Aichner, par. 89, n. 2.

20 *Walter*—"Deutsche Rechtsgeschichte" I, 528; *Gerber* "System d. deutschen Privatrechts," p. 72; Cf. Wernz II, 408.

21 Caroli M. Capit gen. (a 802), c. 13—Boretius, p. 107; c. 29, Conc. Mogunt. 1 (a 813) in Labbe & Cossart "Concilia" VII, 1213, c. 42, Conc. Cabil. (a 813).

22 Cc. 1, 2 X, *de jurepatronatus*, III, 38.

separated from them. The Church, forced by the circumstances in which it found itself, sanctioned lay ownership of churches; not, however, its abuses—in 826[23] and again in 854.[24]

To these abuses, which arose, as it were, spontaneously from the Germanic Law, others were added in the course of time. Kings and noblemen invaded churches, purloined their revenues, gave the churches over to the laity, and even took it upon themselves to appoint pastors in arbitrary fashion. All this was in open violation of canonical principles. It was the application to minor benefices of the false principles which kings and emperors later introduced into the lay-investiture of Bishops.[25]

Finally, especially in England, the ecclesiastical *advocates* appointed for the protection of benefices, usurped the rights of lawful patrons.[26]

A reaction against these abuses was instituted by the Church in the eleventh and twelfth centuries. It had the effect of recalling the right of patronage to its primary and correct use. The principal factor in the reform was Alexander III. He declared the right of patronage a "jus spirituali annexum",[27] thus bringing all competency in regard to it into the hands of the Church, where it rightfully belonged. He declared the ownership of churches by private individuals and abuse,

23 C. 33, C. XVI, qu. 7: "Monasterium vel oratorium canonice constructum, a dominio constructoris, eo invito, non auferatur." Mansi XIV, 1006.

24 As above—note 23—Mansi XIV, 1006.

25 Cc. 4, 23, X, de jure patronatus, III, 38; cf. Kirchenlexicon v. Patronatsrecht.

26 Note: Very often patrons were at the same time advocates, but there was—as has already been pointed out—an essential distinction between them. The patron enjoyed the right of presentation in virtue of his capacity of founder. The advocate was not a founder, and merely had the right to defend the church, not the right to nominate the rector. Advocates still exist in Austria.—Aichner, p. 89; cf. Archiv. IV, 31-32.

27 C. 3, X, *de jud*, II, 1.

and collation of churches by laymen null and void.[28] Further, he forbade clerics to take possession of churches in virtue of an hereditary right.[29] Churches might not be alienated.[30] The authority of the bishop is necessary for the acquisition of an ecclesiastical benefice.[31] The owner of a church has no right to confer a benefice, much less the right to transfer this assumed right to another.[32]

From these decisions of the sacred canons which were based on the former law of the Councils it became evident that the right of patronage arose not from ownership of church property, but from the concession of the church.[32a] The patronal right, as far as the right of presentation is concerned, became simply a right to present worthy clerics to vacant benefices, not a right to institute cleric "propria marte" in those benefices.[33]

The legislation on the Juspatronatus was thus essentially determined for future centuries. As constituted by Alexander III, it passed into the authentic collections of Gregory IX., and with a few exceptions and additions in regard to the difference between lay and ecclesiastical patronage, into the "Sextus" of Boniface VIII., into the "Clementinae" of Clement V., and into the Decrees of the Council of Trent. It constituted the law in force up to the promulgation of the Code.[34]

But the historical development of the right of patronage does not end here. There is another chapter in its history, which it will aid to note. Before we proceed to this chapter, a few deductions may be made from what has already been said.

28 C. 5, X, *de jure patronatus*, III, 38.
29 C. 15, X, *de jure patronatus*, III, 38.
30 C. 16, X, *de jure patronatus*, III, 38.
31 C. 4, X, *de jure patronatus*, III, 38.
32 C. 11, X, *de jure patronatus*, III, 38.
32a Cf. Imbart de la Tour 205-208.
33 C. 24, X, *de jure patronatus*, III, 38.
34 Wernz II, 408.

First, the right which from the eleventh century onward became known as the right of patronage, passed through a long period of development.

Secondly, that the right of patronage, understood as the right to present a suitable cleric to a vacant ecclesiastical benefice, i.e., a *semi-full,* or *imperfect* juspatronatus, reaches back to the fifth century. This the texts sufficiently show.

Thirdly, that the right of patronage was originally only a personal, not-transferable right of the founder; hence, not based on the lay ownership of church property, as P. Thomas[35] contends, since every right of lay-ownership of church property was expressly interdicted up to the ninth century.

Fourthly, that the fundamental juridical basis of the juspatronatus is the concession of the Church. Not as J. Boehmer[36] and his later followers, e.g., Hinschius,[37] wish, viz., the supreme right of the people and Emperor in things ecclesiastical as well as temporal.

This concession, though not expressly stated in the documents, as Vermeersch observes[38] was in turn based upon the traditional sense of gratitude towards benefactors, which the Church had manifested from earliest times, and arose likewise from the desire of the Church to have the faithful construct churches and benefices for the common good of the church.[39]

Later on, i. e., in the ninth century, it is true, the Church, pressed by the circumstances in which she found herself, principally the feudal system of the tenure of property, gradually admitted some vindication of the rights of ownership of church property granted by the feudal system. But this was many centuries after the origin of the juspatronatus.

35 P. Thomas—"Le Droit de Propriete de Laiques."
36 Boehmer II, 321.
37 P. Hinschius, vol. II, 618-701; III, 6-118.
38 Vermeersch II, 775.
39 De Fargna I, 2-5.

Our conclusion must be that the right of patronage originated in the fifth century, that it was originally a personal, non-transferable right, and that its juridical basis was the concession of the Church.[40]

A few more words will suffice to bring the history of patronage up to the present day.

In the later Middle Ages, chapters, abbies and convents obtained many rights of patronage, in view of the fact that these were founded on property owned by them. Many religious corporations came into possession of patronage by legacies, donations, and other legal acts. By virtue of indults, they likewise received many rights of presentation. These were all acquired in agreement with the canon law.[41]

But, since the end of the Middle Ages, the German princes had come into possession of many patronages, which stood in open violation of canonical principles. Of these, the chief ones were those obtained by enfœffment of church goods, and by advocacy. These, in conjunction with the genuine patronages which they had, gave rise to the theory that his Majesty's patronages were based not on canonical grounds, but upon his right of sovereignty, a revival of the old Germanic law, which, as has been seen, was superseded by the authentic canonical legislation of Alexander III.

This idea of the right of sovereignty of rulers was sponsored in France by Louis XIV and by the French canonists; also in Austria, and in Italy, under the general term "Febronianism", and later "Josephism." But it was a most unjust usurpation of the rights of the Church, and a violation of the Church's constitution.

The most flagrant abuses of this assumed right of sovereignty followed upon the suppression of institutes

40 Cf. Archiv. IV, 3-38—Art. by Prof. Rooshirt.

41 C. 1, X, *De capell monach,* III, 37; c. 18, X, *De praescript.,* II, 26; cf. Kirchenlexicon v. Patronatsrecht, n. 1.

42 Cf. Philips "Kirchenrecht" VII, 691.

and convents in Austria, under Joseph II. Here it was claimed that all rights of patronage attaching to those institutes and convents devolved upon the Emperor, and that he was alone competent to confer those benefices. The same was done in the rest of the German Empire upon the secularization of convents in the eighteenth century.[42]

Against such manifest abuses, the Church continually raised her voice. She declared once more that the juspatronatus is a "jus spirituali annexum", and so, with the aid of canonical science and the general consciousness of justice, succeeded in bringing about, by means of agreements and concordats, a favorable settlement of the whole question.

In Prussia and Baden, the question was settled by an agreement between the Bishops and the Governments. In Wuertemburg, by concordat, two hundred places were placed under the free collection of the Bishops, and three hundred and twenty-six under royal patronage. In Austria, by concordat, the Emperor was conceded the right to nominate to benefices of religious or academic foundation. In Bavaria, by concordat, the king had the same right of presentation which the suppressed religious corporations possessed.[43]

Such is in brief the general canonical history of the juspatronatus. A more detailed history, though interesting, would be beyond the purpose of this work. Though brief, the ideas given are sufficient to aid one in the understanding of the new law on patronage, and to vindicate its severity. It is with this intention only that the historical discussion has been introduced.

43 Cf. Saegmueller 286; "Kirchenlexicon" v. Patronatsrecht, n. 1.

CHAPTER IV

Prohibition of Future Rights of Patronage

1—No New Patronages May Be Created

Canon 1450 makes, perhaps, the only substantial changes in the New Law. It is the canon which determines the spirit of the whole chapter on patronage in the Code. It says:

"Par. 1—In future, no right of patronage may validly be created by any title.

Par. 2—The ordinary may however:

n. 1—Grant to the faithful who have either wholly or partially constructed churches or founded benefices, spiritual suffrages, for a certain period of time, or even perpetually, according to the generosity (of the latter).

n. 2—Admit the foundation of a benefice with the condition that the benefice be conferred for the first time upon a clerical founder, or upon another cleric designated by the founder."[1]

This canon is a derogation of the Old Law,[2] that is a partial revocation[3] of the law by which patronage was granted in the older legislation. According to the former legislation, as has already been said in the third chapter, the right of patronage was acquired by the foundation, endowment and construction of a church or benefice,[4] provided the founder, endower or builder obtained the consent of the Ordinary of the place where the church or benefice was located. Thus the Gloss in c. 26 CXVI., Qu. 7, "Patronum faciunt dos, aedificato fundus." And it was the common teaching of the canonists, who based

1 C. 1450.

2 Blat III, 354.

3 Wernz I, 118.

4 C. 26, C. XVI, qu. 7; c. 25, X, d., jure patronatus, III, 38; Wernz II, 414; Saegmueller 280.

their reasonings on the Law of the Decretals[5] and on Trent,[6] that by any one of these titles, with the consent of the Ordinary the right of patronage was granted. Also by rebuilding a ruined or dilapidated church, or by re-endowing a bankrupt church or benefice, the right of patronage was obtained, with the Ordinary's consent. These five titles were designated by the doctors "ordinary primary" (originarii) titles. Besides these "ordinary primary" titles, there were also other "extraordinary" primary titles, such as apostolic privileges and indults, and immemorial prescription, by which rights of patronage were granted. These extraordinary primary titles were not based on the common law; the ordinary primary titles were.[7]

A second class of titles by which the juspatronatus was obtained, with the Ordinary's consent, were styled "derived" or secondary titles, that is derived from and following the primary titles. These titles are enumerated briefly: hereditary succession (whether testamentary, intestate, or legatine); contract [donation, buying or selling of a thing (piece of ground, church, chapel) to which the right of patronage attaches as accessory to the principal]. The secondary or derived titles, therefore, denoted the lawful means by which a right of patronage obtained by one of the primary titles could be transferred to a capable (i.e., recognized by law) person.[8]

The derogation of the Old Law made by this canon is this: No right of patronage may be validly created in future by any of the primary titles given above.[9] Thus the first paragraph of the canon may be explained; no right of patronage properly so-called, such as existed in the old law, and of which we have spoken throughout our

5 C. 32, C. XVI, c. 6; c. 31, C. XVI, Q. 7; C. 25, X, de jure patronatus, III, 38.

6 Sess. XIV, *de ref.*, c. 12; Sess. XXV, *de ref.*, c. 9.

7 Ferraris v. *juspatronatus*, art. 1, n. 20 seq.; Leurin P II, q. 30; Schmalzgrueber, III, 38, n. 52; Saegmueller, 281; cf. Wernz II, 414.

8 Wernz II, 414; Saegmueller, 281.

9 Blat III, 354; Vermeersch II, 780.

dissertation, can by any of the original or "primary" titles which have just been enumerated be created as long as the Code is in force.

The wording of the canon, as it stands, may at first sight give rise to a misconception. The words "ullo titulo," seem to be absolute, and thus to abolish patronages arising from both primary and derived titles. But it should be remembered that first, the word "constitui" must be understood in a strict sense, i.e., be set up anew, or to be created. Also, the Code must be taken as a unit, "sic ut digestus est"; that, therefore, one must examine this canon in the light of the other canons of the Code, and in particular of those dealing with the juspatronatus, and must interpret it conformably to the whole Code taken in its entirety.[10]

Thus, when canon 1453 speaks of the manner in which the right of patronage is lawfully handed down or transferred to another according to the "jus vigens," it presupposes that some rights of patronage continue to exist after the promulgation of the New Law, viz., those arising from derived titles. The same argument is deduced from canon 1470, par. 1, n. 4, where the Code declares that the conditions contained in the instrument of foundation be observed, where these admit the handing down or transfer of the right of patronage. Another argument is found in canon 4, where the Legislator declares his intention to respect the "acquired" rights of others, unless he makes explicit mention to the contrary. The juspatronatus is such an acquired right. Furthermore, privileges are not revoked; they are perpetual unless there be an express declaration to the contrary, and they are to be interpreted *strictly* according to their verbal tenor, and are to be neither restricted nor extended unless it is expressly so stated in the Code. Indults are likewise free from revocation, unless expressly declared contrariwise, from the same canon 4. In the light of these

10 Maroto I, 165.

10a Cf. Rossi "De Paroecia juxta CIC.," 113; Blat III, 354; Vermeersch II, 775.

reasons, therefore, one rightfully concludes that it is not the intention of the Code to abolish rights of patronage arising from derived titles. In this conclusion, the commentators of the new law agree.[10a]

But the Code earnestly wishes that even those patronages which arise from derived titles be abolished. Wherefore patrons are persuaded to renounce them. Ordinaries are to urge patrons to renounce these rights.[11]

The reasons why the Legislator wishes, in the course of time, to abolish rights of patronage are numerous. The chief reason, however, is because of the abuses to which the exercise of this right has given rise. Though the institution of the juspatronatus did much to promote the common good of the Church, especially in the earlier days, when churches and benefices were few, and the people generally were poor, throughout the long history of its existence, it has given rise to an interminable series of abuses, and to unnecessary judicial processes. Also, it is a curtailment of the right of Bishops, to whom belongs by a quasi-divine right the collation of benefices in the Church.[12] Furthermore, it is an exception to the common law and every exception is odious to the legislator. For these reasons, the supreme legislator in the Church has determined to abolish it altogether in the course of time.[13] By abolishing future rights of patronage, the legislator violates no principle of justice. For the juridical basis of this right is the concession of the Church, as canon 1448 declares and "He that can say Yes, can also say No." (Ulpian.) Furthermore, rights of patronage are acquired rights, at most, and more in the nature of privileges than strict rights; hence they can be abolished, even those acquired by primary titles, at the will of the supreme legislator, even without cause.[14]

11 Cc. 1450-1451.

12 Cf. c. 1432; Wernz II, 286.

13 Prümmer, Manuale Jur. Canonici, qu. 433.

14 Wernz I, p. 240, footnote 107; Ferraris, v. *juspatronatus*, art. IV, n. 64; S. C. Conc. 20, Aug., 1887, A. S. S. XX, 338

Paragraph two has two parts. It speaks of the rights which the Code wishes to substitute for the right of presentation, which was formerly granted to founders of churches and benefices. This substitution gives a twofold alternative:

1. Spiritual suffrages (i.e., helps) either for a time or even perpetually (according to the generosity of future founders of churches and benefices), may be granted by the Ordinary to the faithful (i.e., Catholics), who shall have either totally or partially founded churches or benefices.

2. In case the founders shall be unwilling to accept these merely spiritual aids, the Ordinary may grant them the privilege of one single act of presentation, viz., the first time that the benefice is conferred. In this first instance the benefice may be conferred either upon the clerical founder, or upon another cleric designated by the lay or clerical founder.

The spiritual "suffrages" here spoken of are, according to Blat, "Prayers and liturgical functions for the benefactors in question, whether they be living or dead."[15] Such prayers and functions may be any sanctioned by lawful custom, provided they be not contrary to law. Thus would be included public prayers, e.g., public recitation of the rosary for the founder, of the Te Deum, and other special devotions, which, however, must not be contrary to the liturgical law. The privilege is to be interpreted broadly, in view of the new patronal legislation, with due respect to canons 2, 4, and 50.

By allowing in the second part of the second paragraph a single presentation, the Code confines within proper limits the power of future patrons (if new founders may be thus designated) to limit the power of the ordinary collator of benefices, viz., the Bishops. This is again in conformity with the spirit of the whole chapter on patronage.

15 Blat III, 354; Ferraris v. juspatronatus, art. IV, n. 144.

2—Limitations Opportunely Imposed
Canon 1451

This canon, which is intimately connected with the preceding one, says:

Par. 1. "Let Ordinaries see to it that patrons, in place of the right of patronage which they enjoy, or at least in place of the right of presentation, accept for themselves and theirs spiritual favors, even perpetual."

Par. 2. "If, however, they are unwilling to do this, their right of patronage is to be regulated by the canons which follow."

The absence of notes in this indicates that it is new legislation, at least in written law. In the scheme of the Code, the prescriptions of this canon were contained immediately under canon 1452,[16] which deals with presentations made by means of popular elections. The reason of its new position is, no doubt, to give it more prominence, inasmuch as it is given the place of a special canon.

The canon refers to patronages already acquired before the promulgation of the Code. This is intimated by the words "Quod ad preteritum," of the scheme of the Code.

Paragraph one is not a command, but merely an admonition given to the Ordinaries, as a decision of the Pontifical Commission for the Authentic Interpretation of the Canons of the Code authoritatively declares.[17] Its

16 *Schema,* III, can. 29. A copy of the code as completed and corrected was sent before its promulgation to all the bishops and superiors of religious orders who are legitimately invited to ecumenical councils, in order that they might freely express their views in regard to the canons. Catholic Encyclopedia—Supplement—Canon Law, v. Code, p. 22. This copy is called "Schema Codicis Juris Canonici." The changes made in the Scheme were based upon the suggestions of those to whom it was sent.

17 A. A. S. XIV, 633. "Quaenam sit vis verbi 'curent'" canonis 1451, p. 1. Resp.—Verbum "curent" citate canonis declarat ab Ordinariis locorum suadendum esse patronis ut loco juris patronatus quo fruuntier, aut saltem loco juris praesentandi, spiritualis suffragia etiam perpetua pro se suisve acceptent; et hinc patronos, praesertim ecclesiasticos, optime se gerere si hisce suasionibus obsequantur."

purpose is to put into practice the prescript of canon 1450, whereby the legislator has determined to abolish entirely the right of patronage, according to the definition given in canon 1448. In this paragraph, the Church defers to the spiritual nature of her benefactors, who should have no other purpose in view in their charity than the common good of the Church and their own spiritual good. In the admonition here given to the Ordinaries is contained an implicit caution to patrons to heed the behests of their Superiors, and renounce their lesser temporal favors of patronage, or, at least, presentation, for the greater spiritual favors granted them by this and the preceding canon.[17a]

If, however, patrons are unwilling to give up these temporal rights, the legislator does not wish to coerce them. They may retain them, for acquired rights are safeguarded by the Code.[18]

The only words which require an explanation in this canon are perhaps "pro se suisve." These words mean: For the patrons themselves, and for those to whom their patronal rights, either from their nature or by the conditions of the foundation, would descend. Thus, in case one who possesses a juspatronatus hereditarium should renounce his patronal right in conformity with the prescripts of this canon, he could obtain for himself and for those to whom his right of patronage would ordinarily be handed down, the spiritual favors mentioned in the canon.[19]

As early as the year 666 A.D. we find the "jus precum," or the right granted to the founder of a church to have his name mentioned in the public prayers of the church of his foundation. Thus we read in the Council of Emmeritiana, canon 19:[20]

17a Com. Pont. ad Interp. Can. 2 Nov., 1922—A. A. S. XIV, 663.

18 C. 4.

19 Cf. Blat III, 355.

20 Labbe & Cossart "Concilia," vol. VI, p. 507.

"Proinde salubri deliberatione censemus . . . et eorum nomina a quibus eas ecclesias constat esse constructas vel qui aliquid his sanctis ecclesiis videntur aut visi sunt contulisse . . . ante altare recitentur tempore missae."

And in the rubric of the Pontificale Romanum, after the address made to the founder "Deinde Pontifex jubet Deum deprecari pro eo qui ecclesiam construxit et dotavit et pro eo qui eam consecari petiit, et concedit iis partem in omnibus bonis, quae ibi fieri contingent."[21]

In Germany patrons also obtained this right, at least in particular instances.[22]

The Code makes this *jus precum*,[22a] or rather its amplification, the primary right of founders of churches and benefices after the Code.[22b]

Although patrons should be shown deference, even outside the churches or benefices of their foundation, and should be treated with due respect by the rectors of patronal benefices, nevertheless, the patron must not think that he cannot be called into judgment without a special permission.[23]

(a) Popular Elections and Presentations
Canon 1452

In many countries, e.g., in the kingdom of Venice, in parts of Austria, Germany and Switzerland,[24] presentations to churches and benefices are made by means of popular elections. That is, a body of the faithful, such as a congregation, or a town, possesses collectively the right to present rectors and pastors to vacant benefices and parochial churches. Such presentations have grown

21 Pontificale De Ecclesiae dedicatione; cf. Wernz II, p. 187, footnote 137.

22 Saegmueller, 292.

22a C. 1455, n. 3.

22b C. 1451.

23 Schmalzgrueber III, 38, n. 96; Wernz II, 431.

24 A. A. S. XIII, 163; Augustine, VI, 526.

up by custom or by prescription[25] and were not sanctioned by the common law before the Code. Now by the Code they are tolerated, but only restrictively, viz.:

"Popular elections and presentations to benefices, even to parochial ones, wherever they exist can be tolerated only when the people choose one cleric among the three designated by the Ordinary of the place."[26]

The doctrine here proposed is clear enough. Whenever the right of presentation is possessed by a body of people collectively, as for example by the members of a certain parish, etc., in order validly to exercise this right, the people must present one of the three clerics whom the Ordinary shall designate. Thus, if the Ordinary designates John, James and Thomas, the people must choose one of them; a presentation of Joseph would be invalid, even though Joseph were unanimously elected by the people. If the presentation is to be made to a parochial benefice, only those approved in the concursus shall be fit candidates.

Wherever custom—centenary or immemorial—prescribes the concursus for all benefices, as in the kingdom of Venice, the concursus is not abrogated by the New Law, as a recent decision of the Congregation of the Council declares.[27]

The force of the words "even parochial benefices" is this: In view of the severity of the new patronal legislation, all the canons in this chapter of the Code are to be interpreted strictly. Were the word "beneficia" used without any modification, one should have to accept the word in its less odious signification, i.e., as "simple benefices," according to canon 1411, n. 3. By adding the word "parochial," the legislator has removed any doubt as to his correct meaning. But it must be noted that popular elections and presentations are only a toleration; they are not approved, and like other rights of presentation should be renounced by their possessors.

25 Blat III, 356.
26 C. 1452.
27 A. A. S. XIV, 663.

The words "wherever they are in vigor" (sicubi vigent), are added to the canon, as Blat observes, because such popular elections and presentations were not sanctioned by the common law before the Code.[28]

Blat would seem to indicate by the words "quia in jure antiquo non fundatae"—"the jus *scriptum* antiquum." In other words, custom was their sanction, not written law.

The purpose of the present canon is no doubt to abolish popular elections and presentations in the course of time.

(b) How the Right of Patronage May Be Transferred
Canon 1453

This canon determines the present discipline with regard to the transference and alienation of the right of patronage. It says:

"Par. 1. The personal right of patronage cannot validly be transferred to non-baptized persons, to public apostates, to heretics, to schismatics, to members of the secret societies condemned by the Church, or to anyone who has been excommunicated by a declaratory or condemnatory sentence.

"Par. 2. The written consent of the Ordinary is required for the valid transfer of the personal right of patronage to others, exceptions being when the laws of foundation declare otherwise, and the prescript of canon 1470, par. 1, n. 4.

"Par. 3. If the thing to which a real right of patronage is attached pass to any person named in paragraph one, the right of patronage remains suspended."

In the original scheme of the Codex[29] the discipline in regard to the transfer and alienation of patronage was more strict. The original intention of the Legislator was as follows:

28 Blat III, 356.
29 Schema III, can. 730.

"With due respect to the laws of foundation, the right of patronage, whether real or personal, cannot validly be transferred without the written consent of the Ordinary, with due respect to canon 747, par. 1, no. 5.

"Neither right of patronage, moreover, can validly be transferred to infidels, to public apostates, schismatics, members of the secret societies condemned by the Church, or others excommunicated after a declaratory or condemnatory sentence."

The reference to canon 747, par 1, no. 5, says: "The right of patronage is extinguished. . . . If the thing in which it inheres, or the family, gens, or line, to which, according to the bill of foundation it is reserved, is extinguished; in which second case, neither does the right of patronage become hereditary, nor can the Ordinary validly permit the donation of the right of patronage to another."

Comparing the law as expressed in the Code with that of the original scheme, one finds that the written consent of the Ordinary originally was intended to be necessary for the transfer of both the real and the personal right of patronage; now it is required only in the case of a transfer of the personal juspatronatus. Secondly, originally it was intended that if the juspatronatus was transferred to any of those mentioned in paragraph one of the canon, as it now stands, the juspatronatus was thereby lost. By the Code the right still remains, but its exercise remains suspended.[30]

These changes are more in agreement with the older fonts of law and with the teaching of the canonists.[31]

The first paragraph deals with the *personal* right of patronage. Transfer of the personal right of patronage to non-baptized persons, public apostates, schismatics, etc., is not only illicit, but likewise *invalid;* i.e., without any juridical effect.

30 C. 1453, par. 3.

31 Ferraris v. juspatronatus, art. II, Wernz II, 418 sq.

The doctrine contained in this paragraph is new in written law. Since the personal juspatronatus is in the nature of a personal privilege, it is of itself a non-transferable right. But often, by permission of the Ordinary, it became transferable.[32] According to the New Law, the written consent of the Ordinary is necessary for such transfer. For the transfer of the real right of patronage, however, this written consent is not required, as must be concluded from the omission of the word "reale" in the New Law. This omission is a positive one, as is seen by comparing the canon in the scheme of the Codex with the canon as it stands in the Code.

One might conclude, at first sight, that if the real right of patronage be transferred to any of those mentioned in this paragraph, the transfer itself is a valid transfer. Such, however, is only partly true, as is learned from the third paragraph. The transfer of the thing to which the patronage is attached is valid indeed, but the transfer of the right of patronage attaching to the thing remains suspended until such time as the object of the patronage pass to one capable of exercising it.[33]

The reason underlying this first paragraph is that the juspatronatus is a concession of the Church,[34] not a consequence of the ownership of church property, as was once contended in certain parts of Germany, Austria and France. And another reason is that the Church grants favors only to the worthy, "Infamibus portae non pateant dignitatum."[35]

To ascertain who are comprehended under the terms "heretics, schismatics, apostates," recourse must be had to canon 1325, par. 2. By the term "public" apostates are meant those apostates whose defection from the

32 Saegmueller, in Catholic Encyclopedia, vol. XI, 561 a.

33 Hinschius III, 337; Wernz II, 409.

34 Cf. C. 1448; Vermeersch II, 776; Thomas 118.

35 R. I. 87, in VI°.

church is known to many, or of such nature that the knowledge of their apostasy will readily become known to many.[36]

In paragraph 2, attention must again be called to the fact that this prescription refers only to the personal right of patronage. For the valid transfer of a *personal* right of patronage the *written consent* of the Ordinary is necessary. For the valid transfer of the real juspatronatus this written consent is not necessary. The oral consent of the legitimate superior is necessary for the alienation of ecclesiastical things;" Non onmes tamen res ecclesiasticae canone attinguntur, sed eae solae sive immobiles sive mobiles, quae servando servari possunt, quae proin non consumuntur primo usu. Non attinguntur res quae consumendae vel alienandae sunt ne pereant vel quae nullum usum habent misi alienentur; sic per se pecuniae." This even for validity.[37]

(c) Proofs of the Right of Patronage
Canon 1454

In a preceding canon the Legislator expressed his intention to abolish the right of patronage.[38] But it were to no purpose to signify this intention, were not opportune means taken to carry it into effect. Accordingly, in this canon, as in the two which precede, limitations are set up to expedite its suppression and to guard against abuses. Full proofs of the possession of the patronal right are demanded by the canon.

"No right of patronage may be admitted unless it is vouched for by authentic documents or other legitimate proofs."[38a]

Rights are based on facts, and facts should be proved. The juridical facts upon which the right of patronage

36 Cf. C. 2197, n. 1.

37 C. 1530, par. 1, n. 3.

38 C. 1450, par. 1; cf. Prümmer "Manuale Jur. Canonici," qu. 433.

38a C. 1454.

rests are foundation, construction, endowment, Apostolic indult or privilege, or lawful prescription.[39] Unless there be proof of the possession of one or other of these titles, the presumption of the law is against the possession of the juspatronatus.

All ecclesiastical offices and benefices are presumed of free collation of the Ordinary unless the contrary is proved.[39a] If, therefore, one claims the right to present to an ecclesiastical office or benefice, he must prove his claim.[40]

The doctrine contained in this canon is not new. The Council of Trent (to which the notes of the canon refer) decreed that the title by which a jupatronatus was claimed should be proved "ex authentico documento, et aliis a jure requisitis."[41] The New Law repeats the Tridentine discipline "ex integro," and consequently should be interpreted in the light of the Old Law.[42] In view of the severity of the new patronal legislation, however, stricter and fuller proofs would seem to be demanded after the new law.

A proof is the demonstration of the truth of a disputed assertion or fact. A full proof is one which rests on juridical evidence, convinces the judge, and prompts him to give sentence without further investigation. Strictly speaking, a full proof always excludes the contradictory proposition and therefore must be called sufficient in any case; what is full in its kind cannot be fuller. But it remains true that different kinds of proof carry unequal weight and may produce various states of mind, from mere presumption to absolute certainty.[43]

The Code enumerates several kinds of proof.[44] We mention only those which pertain to our subject. Inci-

39 Wernz II, 413-422; Saegmueller, in Catholic Encyclopedia, XI, 560-562.

39a C. 152, par. 1.

40 C. 1432, Wernz II, 417.

41 Sess. XXV, *de ref.*, C. 9.

42 C. 6, n. 2.

43 Augustine VII.

44 L. IV, tit. X, CIC.

dentally, the proofs to which we shall refer are *judicial* ones, whereas the proofs demanded by the canon which we are considering may be either judicial or extra-judicial. But the canons apply likewise to extra-judicial proofs, "congrua congruis referendo."

The chief proofs of the possession of the right of patronage will be documentary proofs,[45] prescription[46] and presumptions of law and of fact.[47]

If during a long period of time, exceeding the memory of man, many presentations have been made, the presumption of the law is in favor of the possession of the right of patronage. This was the law of the Council of Trent.[48] According to the doctors, two presentations or more were sufficient to establish the presumption.[49] Since the Code repeats the Old Law, we think that this still holds good. But in cases where there is a just suspicion of usurpation, fuller and more exacting proofs may be demanded, e.g., a suppletory oath of the patron who vindicates to himself the disputed right and the testimony of reliable witnesses. This was likewise the Tridentine discipline[50] and is "a fortiori" to be demanded after the Code.

The canon treats explicitly of the *right of patronage* as such. It may be asked whether similar proofs may be demanded when one claims merely the right of presentation? We answer: Unqualifiedly, Yes! Because, first, presentation is treated "ex professo" in no other part of the Code; secondly, the reason why such proofs are demanded in case of the right of patronage is precisely *because of* the right of presentation which the patronal right usually contains; thirdly, what is asserted, of the whole, certainly obtains concerning the principal part, viz., the right of presentation.

45 C. 1912-1835.

46 Cc. 1508-1509, n. 6.

47 C. 1825-1828.

48 Sess. XXV, de ref., C. 9.

49 Ferraris, IV v. *juspatronatus*, art. 111, n. 41; S. R. Rota, Dec. 557, sub. n. 1; dec. 139, n. 12.

50 Sess. XXV, de ref., C. 9.

CHAPTER V

Canon 1455
PRIVILEGES OF PATRONS

Canon 1455, which determines the "summa privilegiorum" spoken of in the definition of patronage in canon 1448, has the following:

"1. The privilege of presenting a cleric to a vacant church or vacant benefice.

"2. Provided that the obligations incumbent upon the benefice have been discharged, the expenses of the church paid and the maintenance of the beneficiary provided for, the patron—even though he may have renounced his right of patronage in favor of the Church—enjoys the privilege of obtaining, out or equity, support from the revenues of the church or benefice, as often as he has through no fault of his own become reduced to a state of want.

"3. The privilege of having, where custom permits, the coat of arms of his *clan* or family, of preceding other laymen in processions and similar functions, of having a seat of honor in the patronal church, but outside the presbytery and without a canopy."[1]

The first privilege enumerated, which is the principal one of the patron, was granted by common law even before the Code. It is found in the authentic collection of Gregory IX.[2] This privilege can be traced back to the year 441 A.D. It is the privilege which the legislator dislikes most to give[3] and which he wishes in particular to abolish because of many abuses to which it has given rise.[4]

1 C. 1455.
2 C. 25, X, de jurepatronatus, III, 38.
3 Vermeersch II, 777.
4 Cc. 1450-1451.

The first half of number 2 of the canon is found in Gratian taken from the Council of Toledo[5] and in the Decretals of Gregory IX.[6] It was likewise the common teaching of the canonists that it was a privilege common to all patrons.[7] The latter half of this number of the canon is new, the Legislator's purpose being, according to Vermeersch,[8] "in order to induce patrons the more easily to renounce his right of patronage, or at least his right of presentation." This, it has been seen, the Lawgiver greatly desires. Number 3 of the canon is also found in the Old Law.[9] Certain extensions, however, are made by the Code. To have a seat of honor in the patronal church, for example, was not hitherto granted by common law. But the "jus processionis" was already conceded in Gregory IX's Decretals. The privilege of having the family or *clan* coat-of-arms was sanctioned by lawful custom only in certain places.[10]

Number 1. Since this number of the canon agrees in part with the Old Law, it is to be interpreted insofar as it agrees, according to the Old Law. According to the Old Law, the right of presentation consisted in this, that in case of vacancy in a benefice, the patron could propose to the ecclesiastical superior empowered with the right of institution, the name of a suitable person (cleric), with the result that if the one suggested was available at the time of presentation, the ecclesiastical superior was obliged to bestow upon him the office or benefice in question. Co-patrons with the right of pres-

5 C. 30, C. XVI, qu. 7 (4th Council of Toledo, C. 37).

6 C. 25, X, de jurepatronatus, III, 38; cf. A. S. S. VII, 695; XXI, 536; Lingen & Reuss, Causae Selectae S. C. C. pp. 250, 259; Wernz II, 432.

7 Ferraris IV v. juspatronatus, art. IV, n. 114; Wernz II, 432; Pallotini-Collectio XV v. *patronus*, p. 1.

8 Vermeersch II, 424.

9 C. 25, X, de jurepatronatus, III, 38; CC. 26, 27, C. XVI, qu. 7; cf. Hinschius II, 619, 620; III, 64; Wernz II, 430.

10 Saegmueller 291.

entation could take turns, or each might present a candidate for himself or a suitable presentee might be decided by a vote.[11]

With regard to the one to be presented, if the case was one of a benefice involving the cure of souls, the patron must choose one of those approved in the parish concursus.[12]

The presentation could be made either orally or in writing,[13] but under pain of nullity all expressions were to be avoided which might imply the collation of the office.[14] In the old Law, the time allowed to the lay patron to present was four months, while the ecclesiastical enjoyed a respite of six months within which he could make presentation. (By the Code all patrons, whether lay or ecclesiastical, enjoy a respite of six months within which they can make presentation.) By the Code all patrons, whether lay or ecclesiastical, must present within the space of four months.[15] The interval began the moment the announcement of the vacancy was made. According to the new law, benefices to be conferred after the concursus, the interval begins after the patron has been informed of those who have been approved in the concursus.[16] The Ordinary, in the old

11 Saegmueller, p. 288; Wernz II, 424. Praesentationis jus in hoc consistit ut patronus eum valeat designare inter plures idoneos, quem sibi magis benevisum putat. S. C. Conc. 17 Aug., 1895—A. S. S. XXVIII, 491.

12 Saegmueller, p. 288 sq.; cf. cc. 1462. In places where appointments to parishes are made by concursus, this practice is to be continued until the Holy See decrees otherwise. C. 459. "Utrum ad mormam can. 1462 paroeciae aliave beneficia obnonia juri patronatus laicalis conferri semper debeant per concursum, ita ut patronus etiam laicis non possit praesentare misi clericum 1, legitime ex concursu probatum? Affirmative, si paroeciae aliave beneficia jurispatronatus laicalis sint obnoxia concursui jure particulari, ex. gr. fundationis vel legitimae consuetudinis; secus negative somm. Pont. de Interpr. Can.—A. A. S. XIV, 663.

13 C. 6, X, he his, quae, III, 10; Friedle in Archiv. 23, p. 42; Wernz II, 427.

14 C. 5, X, *de jurepatronatus*, III, 38; cf. 150, par. 2.

15 C. 1457; Cc. 3, 27, X, de *jurepatronatus*, III, 38; C. Un. de jurepatronatus 111, 19, in VI°; Wernz II, 426.

16 C. 1457, Ferraris IV, v. *juspatronatus*, art. 4, n. 39; Saegmueller 288 seq.

law, was the judge of the presentee's fitness. The same holds good in the new law.[17]

With the changes noted, these remarks hold good for presentation in the Code. Occasion will be had for a fuller treatment of the right of presentation in particular in the succeeding chapter.

"Vacant" is to be understood according to canons 183 ff., i.e., in the strict, juridical sense of the term. Thus only by *renunciation* (by one possessed of his reason), by juridical *privation, removal, transfer,* or by the *lapsing of the time prescribed by law;* these are the legitimate means by which an ecclesiastical office and benefice become vacant. A benefice does not become juridically vacant because of the absence of the incumbent for a long time, or if the beneficiary loses his mind, etc. Consequently, the patron has no right to present—much less to try to institute—a presentee during the lawful absence of the rector or beneficiary. For the right of presentation is one of the privileges "contra jus" which, according to canon 67, must be given a strict interpretation.

The second privilege granted to the patron—the right to relief in case of want—was granted already by Clement III, in 1191.[18]

In these words: "For the foundation of a church, the honor of procession is also granted to the founder, and if he be verging towards want, he should be properly succored by the Church, as is decreed by the sacred canons." With this prescript of the Decretal Law this number of the canon agrees; this privilege, however, is restricted in the New Law by two condition, viz., provided that the obligations of the benefice have been discharged and expenses paid, and secondly, that the beneficiary has proper support. For what is obligatory in justice takes precedence over that which mere equity demands.

17 C. 21, X, *de jurepatronatus;* Trent. Sess. 14, de ref., C. 13—cf. C. 1464, par. 1.

18 C. 25, X, de jurepatronatus, III, 38.

This right to support is not "ex justitia" due to the patron, but only "ex aequitate"; there is no obligation on the part of the Church to make restitution in case of failure to provide for the patron, since, as Blat observes, and as we know from the canonical basis of the right of patronage, this favor is "ex gratitudine Ecelesiae."[19]

Saegmueller, writing before the Code, interpreted the right to support in case of need rather strictly[20] demanding that the patron be "so reduced to want that he can no longer obtain the necessaries of life." This, in the light of the new law, is a rather strict interpretation. For the new law permits this right to support to the patrons, "even though he shall have renounced" his right.[21] The legislator does not permit patrons, therefore, to renounce this *useful* right, inasmuch as he does not wish them to have any pretext to retain the right of presentation, which he wishes them to give up.

What the same author says of the other demands of patrons to the revenues of their patronal churches and benefices, however, is to be upheld. Thus, "If (the patron) should claim (when not in the state of want) revenues and rents from the patronal benefice these must have been expressly granted him in the bill of foundation with the consent of the Bishop," as the Decretals and the Law of Trent decreed. A strict proof of the right to alienate the goods of the patronal church or benefice would be demanded of the patron, should he wish to dispose of the property of his patronal church or benefice; a papal grant would have to be proved, before alienation could be permitted.[22]

"Even though he may have renounced his right of patronage." According to canon 72, par. 2, a private person can renounce a privilege which has been granted to

19 Blat III, 359.

20 Saegmueller, pp. 292-293.

21 C. 1455, n. 2, CIC.

22 Saegmueller, pp. 292-293; CC. 1530-1532, CIC.

him in his favor alone. But the patron may not renounce his right to support in case of need, from the express prescription of the canon.

"Nulla sua culpa," otherwise, as Blat[22a] observes, the patron does not deserve compassion.

Lastly, this number 2 of the canon says that the patron retains the right to support, even though the pension reserved in the foundation be not sufficient to relieve his need. The pension can be great or small, "provided it does not impugn the nature of the benefice" (can. 1417, par. 2), and that it does not leave the benefice without a sufficient endowment (can. 1415, No. 1).

Number 3 of the canon enumerates the honorary rights of patrons. The three privileges mentioned are the only ones granted by common law.[22b] There are many others sanctioned either by special privilege, indult, or custom. Of these latter, Saegmueller gives ten which are found especially among patrons in Germany.[23] The most frequent among these are: 1—those enumerated by the Code, and now extended universally to all patrons;[23a] 2—the "jus precum," or right to certain special prayers, which the Code[23b] would seem to substitute for the right of presentation previously enjoyed by patrons. Examples of the contents of the "jus precum" are, the right to special mention in the Holy Sacrifice, special public prayers for the patrons, etc.; 3—the "jus aquae benedictae seu aspersionis," or the right to be blessed before other members of the parish at the "Asperges," not, however, by reaching them the "aspergill"; 4—the "jus luctus ecclesiastici," or the privilege of having the bell tolled at the demise of any member of the patron's family; 5—the "jus cerei et palmarum," or the privilege of receiving first on Candlemas Day and Palm Sunday, respectively,

22a Blat III, 359.

22b Viz.—the right to the geneological record (Stemma) of his race or family, precedence over other laics in processions and similar functions, and a prominent seat in the patronal church. C. 1455, n. 3.

23 Saegmueller, pp. 291-292; cf. Wernz II, 430.

23a C. 1455, par. 2, 3.

23b C. 1450, par. 2.

the candles and palm, etc. Another privilege, mentioned by the Code, is the right of the patron to choose the patronal church as the church of burial. These privileges, granted as they are by indult, or lawful custom, are to be regulated by the laws governing privileges and customs, in the first book of the Code.[24] Since they are not mentioned in the Code—with the exception of the last —the presumption of the law is against them and they must be proved before they can be admitted.[25] Furthermore, they are of their nature odious, in the juridical sense of this term, and consequently subject to strict interpretation.[26]

The "extra presbyterium" clause of the canon is taken from the Decretals, which quotes the Council of Mainz, and reads: "Let not laymen presume to stand or sit among the clergy" (when the sacred mysteries, i.e., the Holy Mass, are being celebrated). "But that part which divides the chancel from the altar is reserved ('patet') for the clerics who sing."[27]

"Sine baldachino," is inserted from a general decree of the Sacred Congregation of Rites, Mar. 13, 1688, which says: "Since the S. C. R., adhering to decrees at other times published, has declared that the gospel (book) is not to be given to the laity to kiss, etc., etc., *and has prohibited the use of the canopy* (baldachinum), etc., the eminent and most reverend fathers of the S. C. R. have commanded that these decrees be renewed."[28]

Wherever, therefore, patrons enjoy the last two named privileges, which are "contra jus," as is seen from the wording of the canon, unless they be of a hundred years standing, or at least immemorial, or granted by papal indult, they are to be considered corruptions of the law, and therefore to be abolished.[29]

24 CIC—L. I, tit. IV, V.
25 CC. 1825-1828.
26 Cocchi I, 118.
27 C. I, X, de vita et honest cleriocorum, III, 1.
28 S. R. C. Decr. Auth., n. 1792.
29 C. 5.

CHAPTER VI

THE RIGHT OF PRESENTATION

The preceding canon gives a general knowledge of the sum of privileges granted patrons. The succeeding ten canons speak of the right of presentation, in particular.[1] This right, as has frequently been remarked, is the principal right of the patron, objectively speaking. It is the privilege which the legislator dislikes most to give; which most impedes the free collation of ecclesiastical offices; which Bishops are urged to induce patrons to renounce; which has determined the spirit of the whole chapter on patronage in the New Law.

The Code follows the law of the Decretals in treating the right of presentation under the chapter which deals with the Right of Patronage, although the new law is careful to distinguish the one from the other. According to the old law, and its commentators, as is seen from the definitions given by the authors, this distinction was not too strictly inculcated.[2] From the Code, it is evident that the right of presentation stands in relation to the right of patronage as a part to the whole. Presentation is the principal part of the patronal rights which had their origin before the promulgation of the New Law.[3] The right of presentation may not be granted to the founders of churches after the new law, except for the initial time that the church or benefice of foundation is collated.[4] But since many rights of presentation will continue to exist for a long time to come, the Code legislates in ten canons its lawful exercise.

1 Cc. 1456-1465.

2 Pirhing, III, 38, *de jurepatronatus*, I, 1; Reiffenstuel, III, 38, *de jurepatronatus*, I, 3; Wernz II, 401.

3 C. 1455, n. 1; cf. Wernz II, 401.

4 C. 1450.

First, the Code considers who may lawfully exercise the right of presentation (C., 1456); secondly, the time within which it must be exercised, and the result of failure to exercise the right within the prescribed time (1457-1458); thirdly, presentation by a plurality of patrons (1459); fourthly, how presentation is made when exercised [a]in collegio, [b]in solidum (C., 1460); fifthly, of the distinction which must intercede between the one who presents and the one presented (C., 1461); sixthly, presentation by means of a concursus (C., 1462); seventhly, of the qualities required in a presentee (C., 1463); eighthly, to whom presentation must be made (C., 1464); ninthly, of the rejection of a candidate, or presentee (C., 1465).

In our treatment of presentation, the order and scheme of the Code has been observed. The effects of a lawfully made presentation are treated in the next chapter, which will deal with canonical *institution*. This is done in order to confine the present chapter to reasonable limits.

There are four principal ways of providing for vacancies in ecclesiastical offices, viz., free collation, canonical institution, admission, election.[5] These are called "modi ordinarii." The generic term underlying them is canonical provision, which is defined by the Code: "The concession of an ecclesiastical office made according to the norms of sacred canons, by a competent ecclesiastical superior."[6]

Canonical provision embraces a three-fold act:

A—The designation of a person to be put into the ecclesiastical office. This designation is either free or not free, according as it is made by voluntary nomination of the ecclesiastical superior, or follows upon the election, postulation, or presentation, respectively, of an ecclesiastical moral person, or patron.

5 C. 148.

6 C. 147, p. 2.

B—The *concession of the title*, or the ecclesiastical office itself, with its rights and duties in spirituals. This concession of the title, when made at the instigation of a patron presenting is called CANONICAL INSTITUTION.

C—The introduction into the actual possession of the office, which is called *corporal institution.*[7]

An ecclesiastical office cannot *validly* be obtained without canonical provision.[8]

With these prefatory remarks on canonical provision, we proceed to the legislation of the Code on presentation.

The Code does not give a definition of presentation. Hence, one, must have recourse to definitions of the doctors. According to Saegmueller, the right of presentation consists in this: that in case of a vacancy in a benefice, the patron may propose (praesentare) to the ecclesiastical superiors empowered with the right of collation, the name of a suitable person (persona idonea), the result being that if the one proposed is available at the time of presentation, the ecclesiastical is bound to bestow on him the office in question.[9] With this definition, the authors generally agree.

Such right of presentation is not confined to minor benefices alone, but likewise extends to major, or consistorial, benefices, e.g., to bishoprics and prelacies.[10] The Code does not limit the present legislation to minor benefices; it wishes to include, therefore, presentations to major benefices in its discipline. It refers to all presentations, to whatsoever kind of benefices or ecclesiastical offices, for it does not distinguish, and in no other place does the Code legislate regarding presentations to major benefices. Since, however, presentations to major benefices are granted usually by Concordats, or by Apostolic indult, and the Code does not regard them unless they be

7 Maroto I, 585.

8 C. 147, par. 1.

9 Saegmueller, I Catholic Encyclopedia v. patron and patronage, XI, p. 560 b.

10 Schulte, p. 675; note 2; Phillips I, p. 328.

expressly mentioned.[11] The present discipline "de facto" therefore has in view especially presentations to minor benefices.[12]

The right of presentation may lawfully be exercised only when a benefice is juridically vacant, that is, vacant according to the norms of cans., 183-195. Not only is the collation of a benefice not juridically vacant forbidden, but even the promise of such benefice is forbidden, and does not obtain any effect when the benefice becomes juridically vacant.[13] This holds even though the promise be made with an oath.[14] Boniface VIII. absolutely forbade all promises, "per quas directe vel indirecte aperiri via valeat ad beneficia vacatura," and declared null such promises, "sub quavis modo aut forma verborum" they were made.[15] The reasons of the prohibitions are given by Schmalzgrueber, viz., to remove the danger of impious desires and counsels, to which such promises can give rise, to prevent the presentation of unworthy candidates, and because of the analogy with the civil law, which prohibits bargaining concerning succession, during the lifetime of a testator, and lastly, because of the harm of such promises to public morals.[16]

For the same reasons, a patron may not grant to any one the *special* power to present a cleric to a definite benefice, in the event of its becoming vacant.[17] But a patron who has several rights of patronage may grant a general delegation to anyone to present to a benefice in case of vacancy.[18] He may not, however, designate a definite person nor a definite benefice. A delegation against these prescripts would be null and void.

11 C. C. 3, 4.

12 Vermeersch II, 779; cf. C. 1471.

13 C. 150.

14 Schmalzgrueber III, 8, n. 30; Wiestner III, 8, nn. 12, 13.

15 C. 2, *de concess, praebend,* III, 7 in VI°; Pirhing III, 8, par. nn. 2, 3.

16 Schmalzgrueber III, 8, n. 21; Pirhing III, 38, sect. 5, par. 1, n. 2.

17 C. 16, X, de concess. praeb. III, 8.

18 Wiestner III, 8, n. 15; III, 38, nn. 79-81; Pirhing III, 8, par. 1, n. 3; Schmalzgrueber III, 8, n. 26.

1—The Subject Who May Exercise the Right of Patronage
Canon 1456

"A wife may exercise the right of patronage without any intermediary; minors may exercise it through their parents or guardians; but if the parents or guardians are non-Catholics, the right of patronage remains for the time being suspended.[19]

This canon deals with the subject who may exercise the right of presentation. The first paragraph was implicitly contained in the Decretals, which referred to an abuse against the juspatronatus by the Countess of Flanders. In the text, Honorius III. implicitly sanctioned the presentations made by the Countess, whose husband was still living, but inveighed against her promising presentations to benefices not yet vacant.[20] The remainder of the canon is based upon the teaching of the canonists.[21]

The doctrine proposed in the canon, concerning the subject who may lawfully present, is not given in an exclusive manner, but merely demonstratively; that is, the canon does not propose to tell who and who alone may present in the multiple kinds of jurapatronatus, but rather decides only the mooted questions concerning the subject who may exercise the right of patronage.

Usually, the founder or his heir, in other words, the one who possesses the right of patronage is the one who may exercise it. But it was formerly disputed whether woman who had obtained the patronal right, and whether children who by heredity or otherwise had acquired it, could present without an intermediary. The Code settles both these questions in the present canon.

It will be of interest to consider the discussion which was had among the canonists in this matter before the Code. From its examination we can obtain another specimen of the severity of the present patronal legislation.

19 C. 1456.

20 C. 16, X, *de Concess praeb.*, III, 8.

21 Wernz II, 424; Ferraris V. juspatronatus, art. IV, 3-8.

The authors were divided into three camps. Ferraris,[22] following Pirhing,[23] Reiffenstuel[24] Garzias,[25] held that children who were over seven years of age could present without authority of their tutors. He argued from the fact that children over seven could validly contract sponsalia. Others, like Schilling,[26] Schulte,[27] Friedle,[28] and Wernz,[29] held that children who had reached the age of puberty could present without any intermediary. This was a very common opinion among the doctors. It was based upon analogous texts of the Decretals. Thus the Decretals granted minors full power to stand in court, without the intervention of a procurator, or "curator": in "beneficialibus et aliis causis spiritualibus."[30] Although the text referred to declared minors self-sufficient only in "beneficialibus et causis spiritualibus," it was so general that other analogous causes could be understood likewise to be comprehended.[31] Wherefore, the authors generally concluded that minors could therefore *present* "per se." Another text, of the Sextus, declared 14 years of age sufficient for participation in the election of a Bishop.[32] But, despite the common view here indicated, there were still others who held to the opinion that only majors (i.e., those over 25, according to the old law), could present without the mediation of the tutor, procurator, or curator, as the

22 Ferraris, v. beneficium, art. III, n. 6.

23 Pirhing III, 38, n. 18.

24 Reiffenstuel III, 38, n. 38.

25 Garzias, De beneficiis, part 2, C. 9, n. 186.

26 Schilling, "Der Kirchliche Patronat," p. 36.

27 Schulte 675, n. 4.

28 Archiv. XXIII, 6-7.

29 Wernz II, 424.

30 C. 3, de jud, II, 1 in VI°.

31 "Si annum quattuordecimum tuae peregisti aetatis, in beneficialibus et aliis ausis spiritualibus necnon et dependentibus ab iisdem ac si major ammis existeret, agendum et defendendum per te vel per procuratorem, quem ad hoc constituentum decreveris, admitti debebis."

32 C. 32, de elect, I, 6, in VI°.

case demanded.[33] This latter view is canonized by the Code. All who have reached their majority, whether they be men or women, may lawfully exercise the rights of presentation.[34]

The scheme of the Code (L. III., can., 733) intended that a wife, whose right of patronage belonged to her dowry, should exercise her right through her husband. This has been changed by the Code, very probably because of the difficulties to which such limitation could give rise. Now she may exercise her right either through her husband, or without his mediation.

Minors are to be understood those under 21 years of age.[35] Minors remain subject to their parents and tutors in the exercise of their rights,[36] except in those things in which the law exempts them from the paternal *potestas*. There is no such exemption in regard to the exercise of the right of patronage.

Since the patron himself or herself must be a Catholic in order validly to exercise the right of patronage, it follows that the substitute, i.e., parent or tutor, should be,[37] for it is unbecoming—to say the least—that non-catholics should take part in so important a matter. There is also the danger of presentation of an unworthy person.

In case of failure to observe the prescripts of this canon, the right of patronage is not lost, but merely remains suspended, either until the minor becomes of age, or until the parents become Catholic.

2—Time Within Which Presentation Must Be Made
Canon 1457

"Presentation, if no just impediment stand in the way, whether of a lay, ecclesiastical or mixed patronage, ought to be made within four months from the day that

33 Lippert, "Lehre vom Patronat," p. 100; A. Mueller, "Lexikon d. K. R." IV, B., p. 381, and n. 4.

34 C. 1456.

35 C 88, par. 1.

36 C. 89, CIC; cf. C. 1648, par. 1, and par. 3.

37 C. 1448.

he who possesses the right of institution has informed the patron of the vacancy of the benefice, or, if it be a question of a benefice which is to be conferred after a *concursus*, of the priests who have been approved in the concursus. But if the bill of foundation, or lawful custom prescribe a *shorter* time, this must be adhered to."[38]

This canon likewise repeats the law of the Decretals,[39] with a slight change. By the law of the Decretals, an ecclesiastical patron, or a patron whose juspatronatus was mixed, had *six* months within which he could make lawful presentation: only the lay patron was limited to the four months' respite. Now, all patrons, whether their patronages be lay, ecclesiastical, or mixed, must present within four months. The severity of the new patronal legislation is once more in evidence.[40]

If the bill of foundation, or particular law, prescribe a shorter time than four months, this shorter time is to be observed. The Church has long insisted upon the strict observance of the time which she prescribes for the filling of such vacancies.[41] But the time is to be taken as tempus utile, and does not continue when one is morally hindered from its observance.[42] Thus, it begins not at the moment that the benefice becomes de facto vacant, but from the time that the patron learns of the vacancy. This was true in the old Law, and continues true in the new. Also, if one is hindered by sickness, by absence, or other lawful reason, from the observance of the prescript of the canon, the time may be prolonged, until recovery, return, etc., as the case may be. A confirmation of this statement may be found in a decision of the Congregation of the Council, of Dec. 17, 1842.

Once the time granted by the law begins, in general, it runs along as tempus continuum, that is, all the days—

38 C. 1457.

39 C. un. *de jure patronatus*, III, 19, in VI°.

40 Blat III, 361.

41 "Mora sua cuilibet est nociva." R. I, 25, in VI°.

42 Blat III, 361; cf. Wernz II, 426.

Sundays and feast-days included[43] must be reckoned, viz., from the time that the knowledge of the vacancy, or the knowledge of the priests who have been approved in the concursus, has been intimated to the patron. It is said, *in general*, for when there is an inculpable and total hindrance of the exercise of the patronal right, the time is broken, "non currit." In case the patron, after a conscientious effort to find a fit candidate, or, in case of a benefice of many duties and few regards, a candidate who will accept, has been unable to present, a longer period of time may be granted within which to exercise his right, years even, if necessary. A decision of the S. Congregation of the Council of Feb. 24, 1720, confirms this observation.[44]

Not all benefices are subject to the law of the concursus, as a recent decision of the Pontifical Commission for the Interpretation of the Code affirms. Curate benefices are as a rule bound to it, but only if the law of foundation, or particular law exact it, is it binding upon other benefices. In this matter, nothing has been altered by the New Law.[45]

Canon 1458

"If the presentation is not made within the prescribed time, the church or benefice become for that turn of free collation.

"But if a judicial controversy which cannot be settled within equitable time (tempus utile) arise either between the patrons themselves concerning the right of presentation, or between the patron and the Ordinary, or between the presentees concerning the right of presentation, the disposition of the benefice is to be suspended until the end of the controversy, and meanwhile, the Ordinary shall, if necessary, appoint an administrator to the vacant benefice."[46]

43 Schmalzgrueber III, 38, n. 218; Schilling, p. 64.

44 Decl. 18 ad Conc. Trid. Sess. 25; I c. 9 de ref.; Richter, pp. 455-456.

45 A. A. S. XIV, p. 663; cf. C. 459, par. 4, C. 1462.

46. C. 1458.

Here again there is a repetition of the old law, this time without any modification.[47] The doctrine was found in the Decretals,[48] and is confirmed by decisions of the Congregation of the Council.[49] The reasons of the canon are culled from the same sources. These reasons are, 1°—that the flock be not long without a shepherd; 2°—because delay is harmful to everyone.

Par. 1.—This paragraph contemplates the case of a presentation which is delayed without a reason sanctioned by law, e.g., negligence, whether inculpable or not. In this case the patron forfeits his right of presentation for that time.

Par. 2.—This paragraph considers those cases, of too frequent occurrence in the past, where a controversy arises either; (a)—between the patron and the Ordinary, e.g., concerning the right of presentation itself; (b)—between the patrons, e.g., as to whose turn it is to present; (c)—between the persons presented, as to the right of preference. In such cases, says the canon, the Ordinary should—if it be necessary—appoint an econome, or administrator, to the vacant benefice, until such time as the controversy is juridically ended. Meanwhile, the right of patronage remains suspended.

47 Blat III, 362.

48 C. 2, X, *de supplenda negligentia praelatorum*, I, 10; C. 12, 27, X, de jure patronatus, III, 38; Thus: (Clement III, in C. 2, X, I, 10) "Nolentes autem, ut status ecclesiae debitus et antiquiis, per insolertiam alicujus subvertatur, mandamus quatenus—nisi praedictae personae (i. e.—regulars) intra tempus in Lateranensi Concilio constitutum, ad vacantes ecclesias tibi personas idoneas praesentaverint, ex tunc tibi liceat in eisdem ordinare rectores, qui eis praesse noverint et prodesse; ita tamen quod ex hoc nullum patronis praejudicium in posterum generetur," Clement III, in C. 27, X, III, 38: "Cum propter discordias laicorum—Fraternitati tuae mandamus, quatemus, si de jure patronatus quaestio emersit inter aliquos; Et ab eo (cui competit) infra quattuor menses non fuerit definitum. Ex tunc ecclesiam ipsam de persona non differas idonea ordinare; ita, quod illi ex hoc non debeat in posterum praejudicium generari, qui jus evicerit patronatus." The same in C. 12, X, III, 38. "Fas tibi sit de auctoria tate nostra appellatione remota in eadem ecclesia personam idoneam instituere, ita, quod ipsa eadem representetur ab eo, qui jus evicerit patronatus."

49 S. C. C. Civitatis Castelli, 17 Dec., 1842; Civitatis Plebis, 30 Aug., 1851, Mantuana, 24 Feb., 1720.

The "lis" referred to in the canon is, according to Blat,[50] a judicial controversy. The econome has similar rights and duties to the vicarii oeconomi in canons 472-473. According to the Decretals, from which this prescription comes, and according to the Code, the administrator is not to be detained in his office after the controversy is juridically ended, and a lawful person is presented.[51]

According to canon 1560, n. 2, causes concerning benefices have a necessary form, viz., that of the Ordinary of the place where the benefice is situated. Under this canon are included causes regarding the provision of benefices, and concerning canonical institution; in other words, all causes regarding the right of presentation have this necessary forum.[53]

It may be asked here, whether the Bishop, or other Ordinary, can in view of the severity of its patronal legislation in the new Code extend the time of presentation?

Since the time within which the presentation is to be made is explicitly determined in the Code, there can be no question of their being able to extend the time in a general manner. They may not. But in single cases, may they do so? For example, if the patron has omitted to present within the prescribed four months, *tempus utile?* There is no special prescription of the Code which

50 Blat III, 363.

51 C. 483; Blat III, 363; Vermeersch I, 422; Cf. C. 4 de officio judicis ordinarii, I, 31: "Cum vos plerumque oporteat ordinationem ecclesiarum differe, pro eo quod quandoque personae vobis minus idoneae praesentantur; aut inter vos et praesentatores, alia de causa radix dissensioniis emerserit—Fraternitati vestae mandamus, quatemus, si quando in vacantibus ecclesiis. vel quia personae minus idoneae praesentantur (this is derogated by the Code), vel alia de causa de jure personas non poteritis in eis instituere; appelatione remota ponatis oeconomos qui debeant fructus percipere; et eos aut in ecclesiarum utilitatem expendere, aut futuris personis fidelibus reservare."

52 C. 12, X, *de jurepatronatus*, III, 38; C. 4, X, *de officio judicis ordinarii*, I, 31; C. 1880, n. 7.

53 Cf. Noval, IV, 72; Vermeersch, III, 17.

determines this question. Since the Code repeats the doctrine of the Old Law, one must have recourse to the old law and its commentators to answer the question.

The answer must be affirmative, "quia his (Ordinariis) jure ad se devoluto in suum tantum praejudicium cedere nuspiam prohibetur."[54] In c. 2, X, de suppl. negl. prael., I, 10, it is not explicitly decreed that the Bishop do this, but the permission is granted him to do so, if he wish; "ex tunc tibi liceat in eisdem (ecclesiis) rectores ordinare." The "liceat," however, only gives the Bishop the right; it does not impose upon him the obligation to exercise the right. "Verbum licet autem non necessitatem, sed facultatem dumtaxat importat."[55]

The time may not, however, be prolonged past six months. Because in the Old Law, even in case of devolution, the time could not be extended longer than six months. In case provision was not made within six months, the provision devolved upon the immediate superior of the Ordinary, e.g., the metropolitan in regard to his suffragan Bishops.[56] This view is supported by the Code.[57]

Incidentally, neither can the Ordinary shorten the time granted by the common law. For, according to the 17th Regula juris, "Indultum a jure beneficium non est alicui auferendum."[58]

Given the occasion, one may here include a few words on the significance of devolution in this matter.

Devolution is understood the transference of the power of providing for a vacant benefice to an ecclesiastical superior, made by the law itself on account of negligence or a crime committed in the provision.

Devolution is full and properly so-called, if the faculty of conferring the title itself is transferred to the Supe-

54 Wiestner, III, 38, n. 97.

55 Schmalzgrueber, III, 38, n. 228.

56 C. 2, X, *de coness. praeb.*, III, 8; Archio, XXIII, p. 40.

57 C. 274, n. 1; cf. c. 1467

58 Ferraris I v. *juspatronatus*, art. IV, n. 31.

rior; semi-full and improperly so-called, if only the faculty of designating the person is transferred to the Superior.

The former is had in granting institution to those presented by patrons, and then the devolution is made to the Metropolitan, according to canon 274, n. 1, if the suffragan has been negligent; the latter is had in canon 1458, which is now under treatment, when the presentation is not made within the prescribed time. Also in canon 1465, par. 1, when a patron has presented two unworthy candidates. Thirdly, in canon 1470, when a patron is deprived of his right of patronage because of a crime committed by him.

The general rules of devolution are the following:

1. Devolution is made ipso jure; no declaratory sentence is required per se.

2. Canonical provision devolves to the Superior under the same conditions that the general or particular law prescribe.

3. If the immediate Superior himself admits negligence or a crime the right of provision devolves upon the ultimate Superior, i.e., upon the Apostolic See, or upon the next higher Superior, in general, in the matter of canonical provision, e.g., upon the Supreme Moderator, etc.[59]

In conclusion, should be noted, concerning presentation in Austria, that custom derived from the Civil Law of that country, sanctions a respite of only six weeks for patrons who live in the country, and three months for those who live outside the country.[60] This custom is still to be observed, after the Code, since the Code sanctions a shorter respite based on lawful custom.[61]

59 Wernz II, 324; Maroto, I, 587 E.

60 Hofdecret 18, June, 1905—cf. Müller, Lexikon. p. 401, vol. IV.

61 C. 1457, "Nisi brevius tampus—vel legitima consuetudine praescriptum fuerit.

3.—Taking Turns in Presenting
Canon 1459

"If several individual persons are patrons, they can agree among themselves concerning alternate presentations, both for themselves and for their successors."

"In order that this agreement be valid, however, the consent of the Ordinary, given in writing, is required; this written consent, moreover, once it is given, cannot validly be revoked either by the Ordinary or by his successor without the patron's consent."[62]

A repetition of the Old Law once more, with a limitation imposed in paragraph two. The "Clementinae" decreed that in order that provision of churches be made easier, we deem it not unsuitable that patrons can freely agree among themselves concerning alternate presentations of a rector.[63]

By "plures" of the canon it is understood two or more, according to the 40th Regula Juris: "Pluralis locutio duorum nunero est contenta."

It must be noted that this canon deals with "singular" patrons, in contradistinction to the collegiate patrons spoken of in the next canon.

If, therefore, the right of patronage is possessed by many individual persons over the same church or benefice, if each possess the right independently of the other, each can present independently of the co-patrons, and in this case, the choice is left to the Ordinary to select the one he deems most fit in the sight of God, among those who have been presented. (C 3, X, de jure patronatus, III 38; Schmalz. III. 38, N 55.)

But, if the patrons wish, they may agree among themselves concerning alternate presentations. Thus, if John, James and Mary, possess independently of one another the juspatronatus, they can agree to let John present the first time after the patronal benefice becomes vacant, James, the second time, and Mary, the third time. That

62 C. 1459.

63 C. 2, de jure patronatus, III, 12, in Clem.

the agreement be valid, however, according to the New Law the *written* consent of the Ordinary is necessary. Moreover, once the agreement is made, it cannot validly be revoked without the consent of the patrons. This consent, too, must be in writing, we think, in order to insure to it a probatory character.

A limitation of the former power of the Ordinary is imposed in the second paragraph of the canon. Formerly, the Ordinary could, if he saw fit, revoke the agreement concerning alternation of presentation, even against the patrons' will. Now, neither he nor his successor may do so,[64] since the written consent which he must give is in the nature of a bi-lateral contract which binds the Ordinary as well as the patrons.

4—Presentation by a Plurality of Persons
Canon 1460

Par. 1. "If the right of patronage be exercised collegiately, he shall be considered the presentee who shall have received the largest number of votes, according to canon 101, par. 1; but if after two ineffectual votes two or more have a larger number of votes than the rest, but an equal number each, all shall be considered presentees.

Par. 2. "If the right of patronage be held by individual persons who have not made any agreement among themselves concerning alternate presentations, he shall be considered the presentee who has received relatively the largest number of votes; if many have the same number of votes, but a larger number than the rest, all shall be considered presentees.

Par. 3. "He who possesses the right of patronage by many titles, shall have as many votes in the election as he has titles.

Par. 4. "Any patron can, before the presentation is accepted, present not only one but many, either simulta-

64 R. I, 1, in VI°; "Omnis res per quascumque causas nascitur per easdem resolvitur"—cf. C. 1549.

neously or successively, within the prescribed time however, and provided he does not exclude those whom he has already presented."[65]

Paragraphs 1, 2 and 4, repeat the older law. Canon 3 canonizes a common view of the doctors.

The first paragraph of the canon considers the case of those whose patronages which are exercised by a plurality of persons in collegio; the second paragraph, those which are exercised by many persons in solidum.

Concerning the former, Celestine III decreed: "Quod in presentationibus Praelatorum (i.e., made by Prelates) intelligi debet (i.e., are presumed) quod fiant de collegiorum suorum assensu, sine quo non obtineat firmitatem. Unde si constiterit Conventus vel majoris et sanioris partis non affuisse consensum, institutiones hujusmodi convenit evacuari."[66] With this the Code agrees. The wording is sufficiently clear, nor of itself does it need any elucidation. But since it refers us to Canon 101, par. 1, a word of explanation may not be amiss. This canon, treating of moral persons acting in collegio says: "Id vim juris habet, quod demptis suffragiis nullis, placuerit parti absolute majori eorum qui suffragia ferunt, aut post duorum ineffacacia scrutinia, parti relative majori in tertio scrutinio; quod si suffragia aequalia fuerint, post tertium scrutinium praeses suo voto paritatem dirimere nolit, electus habeatur senior ordine vel prima professione vel aetate." In other words, as many as three ballots may be taken. In the first and second ballots, he who obtains the absolute majority of votes shall be considered the presentee. Thus, if there be six persons in the collegium, representing the same number of votes, he who receives *four* votes in the first ballot shall be considered the lawful presentee. If, after two ballots are taken, no one receives an absolute majority, in the third ballot the one who receives a relative majority wins. Thus in the case given, if one of the candidates received

65 C. 1460.

66 C. 6, X, *de his quae fiunt*, etc., III, 10.

three votes, a second, two, and a third, one, the one receiving the three votes shall be considered presentee. If in the third ballot all receive an equal number of votes —in the case proposed, two each—all shall be regarded as lawfully presented, and the Ordinary shall choose whom he pleases of the candidates presented.[67]

The rule here given is the general one. If, however, by the laws of the foundation, indult, or otherwise, special rules are to be observed in the acts of a moral collegiate person, these must be adhered to.[68]

All the members of the collegiate body are to be informed of the election.[69] Usually, the information is to be imparted in writing. But if the distance be great, or there be danger in sending the word, this may be omitted.[70] If even one person of the collegiate body has been neglected, he may have the election declared null, unless he wishes to ratify it.[71]

Although all are to be informed, it is not necessary that all be actually present, unless statute-law or custom prescribe otherwise. The validity of the election depends neither upon the presence of all, nor upon the number of voting members.[72]

If one be lawfully hindered from being present, he may not give his vote to a proxy, nor can he vote by letter, unless special law sanctions this.[73]

67 Moroto I, 465-467.

68 C. 101, par. 1, n. 1: "Nisi aliud expresse jure communi aut particulari statutum fuerit."

69 C. 162, par. 1; Cocchi I, 77.

70 C. 162; Cocchi I, 77.

71 C. 162, par. 2; cf. C. 28, X, de electione, etc., I, 6; Schmalzgrueber I, 6, nn. 22-25.

72 *Engel* "Collectio univ. jur. can." I, 6, n. 12: "Si vero aliqui vocati nolint interesse, aut ob impeditum non possint, tunc tolum jus eligendi apud residuos praesentes est, idque etiam *apud unicum* sicut alia collegii aut universitatis alicujus jura etiam in uno conservantur. Hic autem unicus, licet se ipsum ob notam ambitionis eligere nequeat, potest tamen alium idoneum nominare et praesentare superiori." Cf. Ferraris v. electio," art. IV, n. 24.

73 C. 163.

The majority vote must be of those "qui interesse debent et commode possunt." If more than a third of the members of the collegiate body were purposely neglected, the election is ipso jure null and void.[74]

Lastly, the vote should be taken secretly.[75]

The above remarks pertain primarily to ecclesiastical moral persons. Lay moral persons present according to the norms of the foundation, if there be special rules therein; otherwise, the general rules here indicated obtain.[76]

Paragraph two deals, as has been said, with those moral persons who exercise their right of patronage in solidum. The Decretals, quoting the third Lateran Council, said: "praesenti decreto decreto statuimus, ut si forte in plures partes fundatorum se vota diviserint, ille praeficiatur ecclesiae, qui majoribus juvatur meritis, et plurimorum eligitur et approbatur assensu."[77] And Celestine III, in the chapter quoted above decreed: "Quibus etiam (patronis singularibus) ex eadem causa (ut facilius provideatur ecclesiis) permittimus ut plures ad vacantem ecclesiam possint eo modo presentare personas, quod una ex iis eligi per Episcopum valeat et admitti." With these prescriptions of the old law, the new law agrees.[78]

In permitting patrons to agree concerning taking turns in presentation, in the former canon, the Legislator seems to suggest that he wishes moral non-collegiate persons thus to present. But if they are unwilling to agree to take turns, then, the presentation may be decided by a vote. The person receiving the number of votes *relatively* greatest becomes the presentee. Thus, if five patrons, representing nine votes, compose the non-collegiate body, and three candidates are voted upon,

74 C. 162, par. 3.
75 C. 169, par. 1, n. 2.
76 Schulte, p. 672; Arhiv. II, p. 573.
77 C. 3, X, *de jurepatronatus*, III, 38.
78 C. 6, X, *de his quae fiunt*, etc., III, 10.

with the result that one receives *four* votes, the second, three, and the third, three, the one receiving the four votes, i.e., the number relatively greatest—shall be considered the lawful presentee. If all receive three votes each, all shall be regarded as lawfully presented, and it shall be left to the Ordinary to choose whom he thinks the most worthy in the sight of God.

Casting lots to determine the presentee is forbidden.[79]

In reference to those popular elections of which the Code speaks in canon 1452, it must here be remarked that the congregation as such is not a moral person, and has never been recognized as such in canon law. We say the *congregation* as such. By this is not meant the *parish*, i.e., the congregation, or parishioners, inclusive of their pastor. The parishioners in union with their lawful pastor, do form a corporation, or moral person, in canon law.

If, therefore, the parish, in union with its pastor, possesses a right of patronage, this right is to be exercised collegiately, the fathers of the families composing the moral personage casting the votes for the family. Such patronages are frequent in Austria and in certain parts of Italy and Switzerland, and have arisen from the fact that all of the parishioners have taken part in the foundation, construction and endowment of churches, with the consent of the Ordinary. In Austria, and in some parts of Germany, the parish is identical with the political parish, or territory, and by Concordat, the political representative makes the presentation. This is by special law; generally, the political representative of such communities has no part in presentation to ecclesiastical benefices.[80]

Paragraph three of the canon under treatment, states that the patron shall have as many votes as he has titles

79 Decl. 20 ad Conc. Trid. Sess. XXV, *de ref.*, C. 9, Ed. Richter p. 456, n. 20.

80 Archiv. XXIII, 10-11.

by which he has obtained the right of patronage. This, it has been pointed out, was the common view of the canonists before the Code.[81]

Thus, if one obtain a right of patronage by construction and later on by rebuilding, he shall have two votes in the election. If one obtain the right by three titles, he shall have three votes, and so on.[82]

This prescription of the canon under discussion seems to stand in violation of canon 164, which says that although one has the right to vote by many titles, one may not cast more than one ballot. But the difference is only an apparent one. Canon 164 refers to elections strictly so-called, viz., the canonical appointment by legitimate electors, i.e., either clerics or religious—of a fit person to an ecclesiastical office. Patrons, to the contrary, may be layman. Furthermore, this paragraph refers, according to Vermeersch, whose opinion is to be sustained in view of the fact that in case of doubt we must have recourse to parallel canons, *to single patrons* (who exercise their right of patronage not in collegio, but in solidum).[83]

Paragraph 4 of the canon considers what is known among the canonists as the "jus variandi."[84] It states that any patron, whether lay or ecclesiastical, may vary his presentation within the time—four months—prescribed by the law. It thus modifies the old law. According to the old law, only the lay patron could vary his presentation, i.e., could present more than one candidate, either simultaneously or successively. But this variation, even in the older discipline had to take place within the prescribed time of four months, which was granted the lay patron, within which he could make presentation.[85]

81 Wernz II, 414; Archiv. XXIII, p. 9; Schmalzgrueber III, 38, n. 55; Schilling "Der Kirchliche Patronat," p. 49.

82 Wernz II, 414.

83 Vermeersch II, 786.

84 Wernz II, 424; Schmalzgrueber III, 7, nn. 26-27. Archiv. XXIII, p. 44; Ferraris IV v. *juspatronatus*, art. IV, n. 44.

85 C. 24, X, *de jurepatronatus*, III, 38; cf. C. C. 5, X, III, 38; Schmalzgrueber III, 7, nn. 26, 27.

The reason why the lay patron could vary his presentation, and the ecclesiastical patron could not was severally explained by the older canonists. The ecclesiastical patron, they said, has a "jus pinguius, id est ex praesentatione clerici plus juris tribuitur praesentato, quam ex praesentatione laici; firmius enim debet esse verbum ecclesiasticorum quam laicorum"; secondly, the presentation made by an ecclesiastical person is accepted in the sense of an election, or even in the sense of a conferring of the benefice, but in elections there is no right of varying, and therefore, there should be no jus variandi by an ecclesiastical patron; furthermore, it is easier for an ecclesiastical patron to find a worthy candidate, and, besides, he has six months (in the old law) within which to make his presentation, whence they concluded "aequum videtur, ut qui gravatur in uno, relevetur in alio."[86]

In extending the right of varying to all patrons the Code determines authoritatively this point.

Another question which called for much discussion among the older canonists was whether the lay patron had the right to exclude the person whom he first presented, and present a second whom the Ordinary must institute, if he found him worthy. In the terminology of canon law, this question was thus posited. Has the lay patron the jus variandi *privativum,* or merely the jus variandi *cumulativum?* In other words, could the lay patron in the old law present two or more candidates for the vacant benefice of his patronage in such a manner as to exclude those whom he first presented, or could he do so merely in such a way that all should be considered equally presented?[87]

The unbroken custom of the Roman Congregations recognized only the *variatio cumulativa,* and almost all

85a Cf. Pirhing III, 7, *de Institutionibus,* n. 6; A. S. S. XVIII, 570-574, where a cathedral chapter is granted the right to institute a presentee, Schmalzgrueber, III, 7, *de Institutionibus,* nn. 10-11.

86 Ferraris IV v. *juspatronatus,* IV, nn. 55-58.

87 Ferraris IV v. *juspatronatus,* art. IV, n. 44.

the older canonists defended this view, so that Fagnani could say in his day (a. 1700) : "hanc opinionem amplectitur omnis schola canonistarum et legistarum in hac materia loquentium,"[88] nevertheless, a few still held to the *variatio privativa*, especially in later times. Of this number were Schilling,[89] and Phillips.[90] It is needless to re-open the discussion, inasmuch as the Code has decided the question. The "variatio privativa" is not admitted by the Code: "modo ne excludat illos quos prius praesentaverit."

Another question formerly controverted among the doctors, was whether the patron might vary his presentation only once, or many times—as many times as he pleased, provided he did so within the prescribed time? As usual, some held the former opinion, others the latter.[91] The written law gave neither opinion sufficient support. The question was to be judged from the *nature* of the thing, and this holds for the repetition of the variation. For, this comes closer to free provision of benefices by the Bishop than the opposite, inasmuch as the Bishop has more candidates to choose from when a repeated variation is admitted.[92] For this reason, no doubt, the Code has canonized the view of those who admitted such variation, so that now any patron "non unum tantum, sed plures praesentare potest, tum una simul, tum successive"—within the prescribed time of *four* months, for whatever kind of patron, and provided he do not exclude those whom he has previously presented.[93]

To recapitulate, this rather long canon legislates: 1st, How presentation is made when the right of patronage is possessed by a collegiate moral-person; 2nd, How

88 Fagnani, ad c. 24, X, *de jurepatronatus*, III, 38, n. 6.

89 Schilling, p. 73—cf. Archiv. II, p. 412.

90 Phillips, Lehrbuch des Kirchenrechts, p. 346, note 18.

91 Cf. Ferraris IV v. *juspatronatus*, art. IV, n. 46—who gives the authors on both sides.

92 Archiv. XXIII, pp. 47-48.

93 C. 1460, par. 4.

presentation is made when the right of patronage is possessed by a non-collegiate moral-person; 3rd, How the number of votes of the two classes of patrons just given is determined; 4th, The kind of jus variandi which is admitted by the new law.

5—Presenter and Presentee
Canon 1461

"No one can present himself nor accede to other patrons in order to complete for himself the number of votes necessary for presentation."

Just as in election properly so-called, no one may validly vote for himself,[1] so, too, in presentation, no one may validly present himself.[2] Also, as in election, no "collusion" concerning a particular person is admitted, so in presentation, the patron may not add his own vote to that of others to bring about his own election.[3]

The discipline of this canon is taken from the Decretals. Innocent III was asked whether a cleric could present himself to a vacant benefice of his patronage. He answered that since no cleric should interfere with the business of Prelates, no one can present himself to the personage (personatum) of any church, no matter how fit he be, or with what knowledge and other qualities he be endowed. Innocent thus indicated that there should be a distinction between the one presenting and the one presented,[4] which distinction the Code ratifies. The observance of this prescript of the Code is, however, only ad liceitatem; a presentation made in violation of it would not be invalid.

To connive in an election (better, quasi-election) is, however, according to the second part of the canon for-

1 C. 170, CIC: "Suffragium sibimetipsi nemo valide dare potest."

2 C. 1461 CIC: "Nemo potest praesentare seipsum neque aliis patronis accedere ut suffragiorum numerum ad praesentationem necessarium pro se compleat."

3 C. 172, par. 4; cf. also C. 170.

4 C. 26, X, de jure patronatus, III, 38.

bidden under pain in nullity. The patron may not in case of a deadlock in the election add his vote to that of the other patrons in order to complete the number required for his own presentation. For in doing so, he would be the efficient cause of his own election—which is forbidden by the canon. To illustrate by way of example: Several patrons take part in the election of a candidate—let us call one of the patrons A. The electors represent 12 votes, of which A possesses one. The first ballot has been cast with the result that A receives 6 votes and B, another candidate, 6. If A withdraws his vote from B and "accedit allis patronis" in the next ballot, A can obtain the presentation for himself. This *accessus* to other patrons is what is forbidden by the canon. But co-patrons may freely elect one of their number to the benefice of their patronage, provided there be no collusion to this purpose.[5] For hereby, the purpose of the canon is achieved, there remains a true distinction between the moral person presenting and the physical person who is presented, which is the end of the canon. Furthermore, the purpose of the canon is still safe if the patron presents his own son or blood-relation; this is permitted him, for the doctrine proposed in the canon is taken from the old law, and must be interpreted in the light of the old law, which permitted a patron to present a son or blood-relative.[6]

The reason given why no one may present himself is that no one should thrust himself into an ecclesiastical benefice, but should be called to it (by another). "Inter dantem et accipientem debeat esse distinctio personalis," said the Decretals.[7] In other words, the old law regarded the conferring of a benefice as sort of bilateral contract, which involves two juridically distinct persons. The new law retains this idea.[7a]

5 Ferraris v. juspatronatus, art. IV, n. 80; C. 172, par. 1.
6 Archiv. XXIII, p. 34.
7 C. 7, X, de inst. III, 7; C. 26, X, de jure patronatus, III, 38.
7a C. 1437.

6—Presentation After a Concursus
Canon 1462

"If provision to a church or benefice must be made by means of a concursus, a patron, even a lay-patron, cannot present any cleric who has not been approved in the concursus."

The concursus, or "competitive examination," spoken of in this canon derives its origin from the Council of Trent. After the formation of city-parishes in the 10th century, a general principle, whereby ecclesiastical benefices, especially those involving the care of souls, should be given only to those duly qualified to hold them, was adopted by the Church. At first, the criterion of fitness was determined by the canonical examinations for orders. Later (by Innocent III, that great apostle of reform of the 13th century), separate examinations were inaugurated as a means of obviating the abuses that had crept into the prior method of provision. In order to secure greater certainty that only those undoubtedly fitted should be entrusted with the care of souls, the Council of Trent,[8] obliged bishops to assign to each parish a permanent parish-priest, who should know his parishioners. The better to realize this design, the same Council instituted the concursus, a competitive examination to be undergone by candidates seeking appointment as pastors of (canonical) parishes.[9] According to the Tridentine legislation (which the new Code retains),[10] bishops must designate a day for this examination. At the specified time, such as have signified their intention of undergoing this test are examined by the bishop or his vicar-general and by no less than three synodal examiners. All who pass a creditable examination are approved by the bishop. It is from these *approved* clerics (of necessity in benefices involving the cure of souls, *priests,*)[10a] that

8 Sess. XXIV, de ref. C. 18.

9 Catholic Encyclopedia v. IV, concursus 208.

10 C. 459, par. 3.

10a C. 453, par. 1.

the patron must choose his presentee. For the Tridentine discipline, though treating of provision in general, expressly includes canonical provision made by means of presentation by a patron.[11]

Failure to observe the law of the concursus, as outlined by the Council, rendered appointments not only illicit, but even invalid. This is evident from the constitution of Pius V. "In conferendis" (May 18, 1567),[12] as well as from the constitution of Benedict XIV, "Cum illud" (Dec. 14, 1742),[13] which latter is included in the documents incorporated in the Code. If, however, by long usage, or by special permission of the Apostolic See, the concursus may be omitted, the omission does not affect the validity of the provision.[14]

In the concursus, the examiners are bound to consider not only the learning, but likewise the age, prudence, integrity, past services and other qualifications of the competitors.[15]

With these observations on the nature of the concursus here referred to, let us proceed to an exposition of the canon under discussion.

The Code repeats the discipline of the Council of Trent, with a slight change, soon to be indicated.

"Si ecclesiae vel beneficio provideri *debeat* per concursum." Not all churches and benefices are subject to the concursus.[16] In general, parish-churches are as a rule subject to it.[17] The presumption of the law is, therefore, in favor of the concursus for parish-churches, which presumption yields to direct proof to the contrary. In the United States—where, however, the right of patronage does not exist—only one parish in every ten is

11 Sess. XXIV, de ref., C. 18.

12 See "CIC *Fontes* I, p. 212.

13 CIC Document IV.

14 Cf. Acta et Decreta Conc. Plan. Baltimorensis III, n. 40.

15 Cocchi II 11, 338; C. 459, par. 2.

16 A. A. S. XIV, 663.

17 Catholic Encyclopedia, vol. IV, p. 209 c; cf. 459.

subject to the concursus.[18] In Bavaria, presentations to parishes and to curate benefices are in virtue of concordat bound to the concursus.[19] In Italy, parish-churches subject to the right of patronage are subject to it.[20] The same obtains in the two Sicilies, by concordat.[21] In every case, the particular law must be consulted. It will be the determinant.

Shortly after the promulgation of the Code, some difficulty seems to have arisen concerning this canon. One finds the Commission answering this query: "Must parishes and other benefices subject to lay-patronage, according to canon 1462, always be conferred after a concursus, so that a lay-patron may not present any cleric who has not been approved in the concursus?" To this the Commission replied: "Affirmatively, if parishes or other benefices are by particular law subject to the concursus; otherwise, negatively."[22]

From this decision, one can see that the Code does not, by this canon extend the force of the law of the concursus, but merely wishes that things remain as they were before the Code. If, by particular law—or by the bill of foundation, indult, or the like—the concursus is prescribed, then the concursus is not to be omitted; nothing is innovated in this matter by the present canon.

The doubt just referred to seemed to be based on the words, "etiam laicus," of the canon, which were a restriction of the Tridentine legislation. Formerly, the lay-patron was not bound generally to present one approved in the concursus, provided he presented a worthy candidate.[22a] According to the Code, which derogates the law of Trent in this point, even the lay-patron is bound to present only such candidates as have been lawfully approved in the concursus.[23]

18 Conc. Plen. Baltimorense III, n. 40.
19 Concordat, art. 11, a. 1817—Raccolta di Concordati, p. 595.
20 Concordat, art. 12, a. 1803—Raccolta di Concordati, p. 570.
21 Concordat, art. 11, a. 1818—Raccolta di Concordati, p. 625.
22 A. A. S. XIV, p. 663—Com. Pont. de Interp. Can. 12 Nov., 1922.
22a Wernz II, n. 829, ad II, footnote n. 44.
23 Blat III, 366.

In concluding this canon, attention is called to canons 3, 459, par. 4, and 399, par. 2, which come into play here.

Canon 3 warns that the canons of the Code: "Codicis canones initas ab Apostolica Sede cum variis nationibus conventiones nullatenus abrogant aut iis aliquid obrogant: eae idcirco perinde ac in praesens vigere pergent, contrariis hujus codicis praescriptis minime obstantibus." Where concordat-law, therefore, demands or excuses from the law of the concursus, the law of the concordat obtains precedence over the general law of the Code.

Canon 459, par. 4, determines the form of concursus to be observed: "In regionibus in quibus paroeciarum provisio fit per concursum sive specialen ad norman const." Benedicti XIV. "Cum illud," "donce sedes Apostolica aliud decreverit." The word "provisio" of the canon includes presentation.[24]

Canon 399, par. 2, observes that a theological or penitentiary prebend should not be conferred unless there be evidence of the uprightness of life, morals and learning of the candidate, and that—wherever it is required (viz., by particular law or custom, etc.), the law of the concursus is to be observed. Thus, in case of presentation by a patron to such prebend, the patron may present only such as have been approved in the concursus, if the prebend to which he presents be bound to the concursus.

Recourse from the decisions of the Bishop in providing for beneficc conferred after a concursus, are made to the Metropolitan, or to the Holy See.[25]

7—Qualities Required in a Candidate
Canon 1463

This canon, which deals with the qualities required in a candidate, and with the time when those qualities must be present, says:

24 C. 148; cf. Cocchi I, 61.

25 "Cum Illud"—Document IV in CIC, par. 17; Cocchi II 11, 338.

"The person presented must be fit, that is on the very day of presentation, or at least of acceptation, endowed with all the qualities which common or particular law, or the bill of foundation require."

The substance of the canon is taken from the legislation of the Council of Trent.[26] Whereas, however, the Tridentine Synod expressly exempted from this examination as to fitness those presented by a university or college of general studies, the Code omits to do so. The words of the Council of Trent were as follows: "Praesentati, seu electi, vel nominati a quibusvis ecclesiasticis personis, etiam Sedis Apostolicae Nuntiis, ad quaevis ecclesiastica beneficia non instituantur, nec confirmentur, neque admittantur, etiam praetextu cujusvis privilegii, seu consuetudinis, etiam ab immemorabili tempore praescriptae, nisi fuerint prius a locorum ordinariis examinati, et idonei reperti. Et nullo appellationis remedio se tueri possit, quominus examen subire teneatur. Praesentatis tamen, electis seu nominatis ab universitatibus, seu collegiis generalium studiorum exceptis."[27]

Blat contends that this omission (of universities and colleges of general studies) is "fortassis ob inutilitatem."[28] With this we do not agree. Rather, the silence of the Code is a positive silence, by which the Legislator wishes to include also universities and colleges of general studies. For, first, this interpretation is more in conformity with the rigor of the new patronal discipline. Secondly, even universities and colleges of general studies are not immune from the presentation of unworthy candidates. All, therefore, whether presented by a physical or by a moral person, are subject to the examination as to fitness. In this connection, however, one must remember the prescript of canon 459, par. 2, referred to in the footnotes to the canon, by which those whose *knowledge* is testified to either by an academic degree, or by the

26 Sess. VII, de ref., C. I, 3; Sess. XXV, de ref., C 9.
27 Sess. VII, de ref, C. I, 3.
28 Blat III, 367.

office which they possess, e.g., a professor of theology or canon law in a seminary, can be dispensed from the examination as to knowledge. They cannot be dispensed from the examination as to age, prudence, morals, etc.

The qualities required in the presentee are: 1st. Those demanded by the common law.

(a) He must be born of lawful marriage or, better still, he must be a legitimate child. "Legitimi *praesumuntur* filii qui nati sunt saltem post sex menses a die celebrati matrimonii, vel intra decem menses a die dissolutae vitae conjugalis."

(b) He must have attained the age required by law. Thus, e.g., 24 years completed for a pastor; 30 years for a Canon penitentiary, etc. (Can. 453, par. 1; Can. 399, par. 1).

(c) He must have the required mental qualities, necessary knowledge, prudence, experience, etc.

(d) He must have the necessary moral qualities, i.e., true faith, upright life and freedom from grave bodily defects. Thus, heretics, and "fautores heresis," "receptores et defensores heresis," schismatics, excommunicated persons, after a declaratory sentence, suspended persons, interdicted persons and those who are irregular, are excluded.[29]

These demands of the common law may be somewhat modified by particular sanctions,[30] either of particular law or peculiar law, or the law of foundation. Thus, the law of foundation may prescribe that a "beneficium non-curatum" be conferred only upon a priest, or only on a blood relation of the founder. Similarly, a diocesan statute, or local observance, or Concordat-law may demand particular qualities. In the concordats between the Holy See and Austria, and between the Holy See and

29 Maroto I, 588-591.

30 E. G. "Statuta et observantiae"—Decl. 17 Cong. Conc. Richter, p. 352.

Bavaria, it is prescribed that a canon must be a priest.[31] By the concordat with Hanover, a canon must be 30 years old.[32] Sometimes, also, by the special legislation of concordats, the person presented must be indigenous to the place of the benefice, or several years' experience in the direction of souls is demanded.[33] In other places the presentee must be pleasing to the civil magistrate.[33a]

The question here naturally arises whether the presentation of a person who has not the special qualities exacted by special law is invalid, even though no one registers an objection against the provision. Schmalgrueber distinguishes in his answer to the question. His distinction is this: "An certa qualitas in clerico praesentando exposcatur *favore personarum,* preditarum tali qualitate, e.g., consanguineorum fundatoris, aut oriundorum ex certa familia, loco, provincia: an contra qualitas certa e.g. juridici exigitur *favore ipsius ecclesiae vel beneficii,* ut scilicet isti de persona magis idonea provideatur vel illius obligationibus melius satisfiat." In the first, he says, "non ignorantibus et non contradicentibus illis," who should present, the presentation is valid; "quia quilibet favori pro se principaliter introducto renuntiare potest et in tali casu eidem actu censentur renuntiare, qui ita tacent." If the latter, the presentation is invalid, even though no one contradict it, for no private person may renounce a privilege granted in favor

31 Concordat, art. 22, a. 1855, Raccolta di Concordati, p. 826. Concordat, art. 10, a. 1817, Raccolta di Concordate, p. 594. We do not venture to state how many of the 133 Concordats included in the Raccolta are still in vigor. It suffices for our purpose that the Holy See has not explicitly revoked—with the consent of the second parties—those which we cite.

32 Concordat a. 1824, Racollta di Concordati, p. 691.

33 Concordat with Austria, art. 22, a. 1855, Raccolta, p. 826. Cf. Com. Pont. ad Can. Interpr. 26, Nov., 1922, A. A. S. XV, 128, "Salva contraria fundationis lege, et firmo praescripto can. 3 et 1435, par. 3, ita tamen ut etiam in his casibus si nullus inter indigenas reperiatur idoneus seu dignus, canonicatus conferri possint ac debeant aliis idoneis et dignis, ad normam cit can. 404.

33a Littera Apostolica ad Episcopos Austriac—Moy. *Archiv.* I, p. 27.

of a community. "Poterit," he concludes, "igitur ejusmodi praesentatio, nemine petente, ab institutore ordinario rejici."[34]

The words of the canon, "from the very day of presentation, or at least from the day of acceptation" of the presentation by the candidate, indicates the time at which the presentee must have the requisite qualities.

Formerly this question was much mooted among the canonists. According to some[35] the presentee should possess the requisite qualities at the time the benefice became vacant. The sponsors of this opinion rested their claim upon a prescript of Boniface VIII, according to which one in whose favor a general papal indult had been granted could not be given a benefice until he had reached the prescribed canonical age. "Ei cui provideri mandatur simpliciter de praebenda proxime vacatura, sacerdotalis praebenda conferri non potest, si nondum in aetate tali existat, quod possit ad sacerdotium promoveri. Sed aliam exspectare debebit."[36] From this one could conclude that the necessary qualities must be present at the very time of the *vacancy* of the benefice. But in this text there is a question of a papal *gratia expectativa*, which is an exceptional case, for ordinarily only *after the vacancy* occurs is there room for presentation. One may not deduce from an exceptional case a general law.

Schilling and others distinguished.[37] If the necessary qualities were demanded by the *common law*, then it was sufficient that those qualities be present at the time of presentation; if, by *particular* law (of the foundation, statute or observances) it was necessary that the qualities be present at the time the vacancy occurred. Because, they said, the common law prescribes only

34 Schmalzgrueber III, 38, nn. 176-177.

35 Reiffenstuehl III, 38, n. 71, et ref.; cf. Ferraris IV de jurep. IV, n. 71.

36 C. 29, *de praeb*, III, 4, in VI°.

37 Schilling, p. 54; cf. Gerlach "Das Praesentationsrecht auf Pfarrerein," 40.

general qualifications, particular law, very special qualifications. Those who have not the general requirements at the time the vacancy occurs, but who will have them before the time for presentation has expired, may be presented; but those who have not the special requirements of particular law may not even be considered in the presentation. This reasoning was very ingenuous and amounted to a begging of the question. For the patron in either case did not have to present at the moment the vacancy occurred; it was sufficient that the presentation be made within the prescribed time of four or six months, according to the nature of the patronal right.

Others, like Ferraris[38] and Gerlach,[39] were of the opinion that the presentee must have the requisite qualities *by the time that the respite of presentation expired,* so that if one who at the *moment* when he was presented had not, e.g., the required age, but by the time that the period of grace within which presentation must be made, scil. four months or six months respectively for a lay-patron and an ecclesiastical patron, the candidate would have the necessary age, he could be validly presented.

Others still demand that *at the very moment* that the presentation was made, the candidate should have all the necessary qualifications,[40] so that without the consent of the Ordinary such a presentation would be invalid. And should the Ordinary refuse his consent, the patron would lose his right of presentation for that time, provided the respite granted him by law had expired and the patron could not present another.

The Code canonizes this last view, but substitutes "day" for "moment." The necessary qualities, according to the Code, must be present "ipso praesentationis vel saltem acceptionis die." The words "vel saltem acceptionis" leave to the Ordinary the liberty of deferring the accep-

38 Ferraris IV v. *juspatronatus,* art. IV, nn. 70 seq.

39 Gerlach—as in (37)—p. 41; Archiv. XXIII, p. 24.

40 Schulte "System," p. 694; Aichner, p. 285; Phillips, p. 343,

tation of the presentation, if necessary, until the time prescribed by the law has expired. "Acceptation," therefore, does not refer to the acceptation by the candidate, of whom in canon 1436: "Beneficium ecclesiasticum clerico invito et provisionem non expresse acceptani valide conferri nequit," but, as we have said, to the acceptation of the presentation by the Ordinary.

8—To Whom Presentation Must Be Made
Canon 1464

"The presentation is to be made to the Ordinary of the place, whose office it is to judge whether the person presented is fit.

"In order to form his judgment the Ordinary should, according to the norm of canon 149, diligently inquire concerning the person presented and, if necessary, adopt secret measures of investigation.

"The Ordinary is not obliged to make known to a patron his reasons for rejecting a candidate."[41]

The *first paragraph* is found in many places in the Decretals.[42] It is also contained in the decrees of the Council of Trent.[43] Another repetition, therefore, of the old law. The *second paragraph* is but a part of the general law laid down in canon 149 of the Code, which is likewise drawn from the Decretals and the Tridentine law. The third paragraph is new, at least,[44] as general law; it is based on the decisions of the Congregations.

41 C. 1464.

42 C. 6, C. XVI, q. 2; c. 3, X, de institutionibus, III, 7; cc. 4, 5, 8, 10, etc., X, *de jure patronatus*, III, 38.

43 Sess. XIV, *de ref.*, C. I, 3. "Non liceat praeterea patrons cujusvis privilegii praetextu, aliquen ad beneficia sui patronatus, nisi episcopo loci Ordinario ad quem provisio, seu institutio ipsius beneficii, cessante privilegiis, jure pertineret, quoquo modo praesentare; alias praesentatio ac institutio, forsan secutae, nullae sunt et esse intelligantur."

44 Some authors held that the Ordinary must make known the reasons why he rejected a candidate. They based their opinion upon a letter of Alexander III, who prescribed this in a particular case. (Alex. III, in Conc. Later. III, Appendix 1, ep. 37—in Labbe et Cossart "Concilia," vol. X, p. 1274); *Schilling*, p. 393, note 3; Archiv. XXIII, p. 22.

The purpose of presentation is to effect the canonical institution of the one presented. Regularly the diocesan Bishop is the one in whom rests the power to institute clerics.[45] Presentation, therefore, as a rule, must be made to him; otherwise the presentation is invalid. Benefices subject to the right of lay or mixed patronage are not reserved, unless there be express mention to the contrary.[46]

The Code mentions the Ordinary of the place. According to canon 198 this includes, besides the Roman Pontiff, the diocesan Bishops, Abbots and Prelates nulius, Vicars-general, administrators of dioceses, Vicars and Prefects-apostolic, and those who by prescript of the law or approved custom take the place of those just mentioned in the absence of the latter. The major-superiors of clerical exempt religious orders do not fall under the heading Ordinaries of place.

Since the right of patronage does not, as a rule, obtain in places not canonically erected into dioceses, the Abbots and Prelate nullius and the Vicars and Prefects-apostolic do not particularly concern us.[47] Vicars-general cannot confer benefices without a special mandate of the Ordinary; neither can they institute clerics without this special mandate. They cannot, therefore, accept presentations without the same, since the acceptation of a presentation gives a candidate a jus ad rem to canonical institution.[48] Apostolic Administrators may accept presentations.[49] Also, those who by prescript of the law

45 C. 152; cf. C. 1432.

46 C. 1435, par. 2.

47 Wernz II, 411.

48 C. 1432, par. 2; C. 1455, par. 2. In the Decretals (c. 3, X, de inst. III, 7) the Vicar-general, since he was the personal representative of the Bishop, could institute presentees. Therefore, concluded the authors—rightfully, indeed—that he could accept presentations. But, according to the Code, institution is no longer granted the Vicar-general without a *special* mandate. Therefore, neither can he accept presentations. Cf. *Archiv.* XXIII, 41 seq.

49 Cc. 314-316.

or by approved custom take the place of Ordinaries, provided they have the power to confer benefices from their letters of appointment, during the absence or lack of a Bishop or others, may validly receive the presentation made by patrons.[50]

Secret investigations are permitted by par. 2 of the canon. Such secret investigations are necessary in certain circumstances, particularly where the Ordinary has reasons unknown to the patron to suspect the lack of fitness in a candidate.

The reason of the third paragraph is evident. If a candidate is rejected as unfit, it might harm his reputation to reveal the reasons of his rejection. This will not happen in all cases, of course. Wherefore, the canon says that the Ordinary is not *obliged* to give his reasons for rejecting a presentee. He may do so if he wish, or reasonably can. Conscience is to be his guide in this, as in many other places in the Code.

The Code does not consider how presentation is to be made. According to the Old Law this could be done either orally or in writing.[51] From parallel canons the written form would seem to be preferred by the New Law.[52] The presentation can be made directly by the patron or through his representative.[53] The presentation is perfected when the Ordinary to whom the right of institution belongs has received word of it, "si pulsaverit aures Episcopi"; and has accepted it; until that time the presentation can be revoked.[54] The letter of presentation may be given to the Ordinary personally by the patron or by the candidate. A personal introduction to the Ordinary is not required. The presentation can be made at any time within the four months prescribed by the law, and on any day, "cum sit actus

50 Cc. 431-432.

51 C. 6, X, *de his quae fiunt Prael*, III, 10; Wernz II, 427; Archiv. XXIII, p. 41.

53 C. 159; Schmalzgrueber III, 38, n. 114; Wernz II, 427.

54 Archiv. XXIII, 42.

extra-judicialis sapiatque spiritualitatem."[54] Also, it can be made in any place the Ordinary happens to be, for the same reason.[55]

But, in the presentation, all wording which would imply a conferring of the benefice by the patron is to be avoided. A presentation made in such a manner as to imply this would be invalid.[56]

Finally, there must be no simony in the presentation, which would be the case, "quando aliquid datur vel promittur pro habendis vocibus seu praesentationibus patronorum,[57] quamvis id fiat etiam quo ipso praesentato ignorante."[58] For the right of patronage is a "jus spirituali annexum," and may not be misused for the purpose of material gain.[59] Presentation tainted with simony is null and void, ipso jure.[60]

In cases of doubt as to the proper manner of presenting, the Ordinary is the judge. His decision must be followed.

9—What If an Unfit Person Be Presented? Canon 1465

The last canon of this chapter on the right of presentation as such answers this question. It says:

"If the presentee is not found fit, the patron may present another within the time which is alotted him by canon 1457, provided the 'tempus utile' granted him to present has not through the patron's fault expired: but if even the second is not found suitable, the church or benefice becomes for that time of free disposal, unless

55 Schmalzgrueber III, 38, nn. 115-118; Archiv. XXIII, 42; Wernz II, 427.

56 Wernz II, 427; Schulte "System," 698—The words which may be used are: nomino, offero, praesento.

57 C.C. 12, 19, X, *de simonia*, V. 3.

58 C. 27, X, *de simonia*, V, 3; cf. Ferraris IV v. *juspatronatus*, art. IV, n. 20.

59 Conc. Trid. Sess. XXIV, *de ref.*, C. C. 14-18; Sess. XXV, *de ref.*, c. 9.

60 C. 1465, par. 2; cf. cc. 727-730.

the patron has recourse to the Apostolic See within ten days from the judgment of the Ordinary; pending answer, the disposition of the benefice is to be suspended until the end of the controversy; and meanwhile, if necessary, the Ordinary will put an econome—or administrator—in the vacant church or benefice.

"A presentation tainted with simony is ipso jure invalid and renders institution perchance subsequent to it void."[1]

The doctrine of the first paragraph is found in many parts of the old law.[2] The principle underlying the canon is thus enunciated by Trent: "Ad haec liceat Episcopo, praesentatos a patronis, *si idonei non fuerint*, repellere."[3] The Tridentine legislation was, in turn, based upon a chapter of the Decretals, in which Alexander III thus replied to the Archbishop of York: "Quod autem consulis, si clericus idoneus ad vacantem ecclesiam praesentatus, non fuerit a Episcopo diocesano admissus, et postmodum alius idoneus praesentatus, et institutus ab episcopo, possessionem corporalem tenuerit; an primo clerico ecclesiam petente, debet posterior removeri, vel posterior priori praeferri. Dubium non est, qui quin in casu isto melior est conditio possidentis; quoniam antequam praesentatio per diocesanum episcopum approbetur, ratum non est quod a patrono fuerit inchoatum."[4]

The purpose of the canon is, therefore, to make provision for the presentation of none but worthy candidates. The judge of the candidate's fitness is the Ordinary of the place. If, then, the Ordinary cannot consciously accept the person presented, he may, without manifesting his reasons to the patron,[5] ask the patron to present a second candidate. If this second be found unfit the patronal church or benefice become for that time for free disposal. If the patron feel that he has

1 C. 1465.

2 Cc. 5-28-29, X, *de jure patronatus*, III, 38, etc.

3 Sess. XXV, *de ref.*, C. 9.

4 C. S., X, *de jure patronatus*, III, 38.

5 C. 1464, par. 3.

been injured, he may have recourse from the judgment of the Ordinary. The recourse is to the Apostolic See, viz., to the Congregation of the Council,[6] not to the next Superior, e.g., Metropolitan or Apostolic Delegate. The conclusion is that the recourse is made *only* to the Holy See, and to an inferior, from the fact that in the Code,[7] in the canon which corresponds to the one treated, the words, "Ad Apostolicam Sedem," were omitted. The reason underlying this prescription of the canon is this: The Bishop may have maliciously rejected a candidate; the Bishop may therefore be guilty of a crime, and consequently must be judged by the Holy See, who is alone competent in cases of Bishop *quoad criminalia*, (Can. 1577, par. 1, no. 3.) Their insertion in the Code was made to avoid ambiguity as to whom the recourse must be had. The recourse to the Holy See is proposed "taxative"; recourse to an inferior would be without effect.

The recourse is to be interposed within ten days, and the Ordinary should be informed that it has been made. Should the Ordinary confer the church or benefice upon another *within* ten days after he has rejected a candidate, the provision would not be invalid, but could be rescinded; after ten days, provided he has not been informed that recourse has been made, the provision is valid and not rescindible.

Ordinarily, the patron may make as many presentations as he wishes, provided he do so within the prescribed time of four months. But if he present *two unworthy* candidates, his right of presenting is for that

6 C. 250, par. 2.

7 L. III Canon and 42, par. 1: "Si praesentus hand idoneus fuerit repertus, patronus, dummodo tempus utile ad praesentandum lapsum ne sit, potest alium intra tempus de quo in can. 734 (i. e. canon 1457, of the Code) praesentare; sed si ne hic quidem idoneus repertus fuerit, ecclesia vel beneficium pro eo casu fit liberae collationis, nisi patronus vel praesentatus intra decem dies a significatione recusationis recursum *a judicio Ordinarii interposuerint;* quo pendente, servetur praescriptum, canon 735, par. 2 (i.e. canon 1458, par. 2, of the Code).

time suspended.[8] Only *two* presentations are granted him in this case, unless the Sacred Congregation of the Council permit by its decision, in case of recourse, a third presentation; but very probably, if not certainly, not more than three presentations, lest the appointment to the benefice be deferred too long, with its consequent harm to the Church.

Paragraph 2 recalls the sad history of abuses to which the right of patronage has ever been exposed. Among the many abuses—protracted law-suits, long vacancies in churches, etc.—simony has been of most frequent occurrence. Whence, the canon decrees: "Praesentatio, labe simoniaca infecta, est ipso jure irrita, et etiam institutionem forte subsecutum irritam reddit."

Although a declaratory sentence is required that the patron be thought to have lost his right of patronage by a simoniacal presentation,[9] such sentence is not required to declare the *presentation itself* void. This happens ipso jure, if simony has taken place; on this point the canon is clear.

The simony referred to may be either or divine law, or of ecclesiastical law. To judge concerning the simony recourse must be had to canons 726 to 730. Simony will be discussed fully in the treatment of canon 1470; it will suffice simply to make mention of the canons here.

8 C. 1465, par. 1.

9 C. 1470, par. 3.

CHAPTER VII

CANONICAL INSTITUTION

In the law of the Decretals, canonical institution was treated under the heading of a distinct chapter.[10] The Code deals with it under the chapter on the right of patronage, or, more specifically, immediately after the canons which consider the right of presentation. The innovation makes for better order, inasmuch as canonical institution is a direct effect of a presentation lawfully made and accepted by the competent ecclesiastical superior.[11] Canonists, therefore, welcome the new position of this legislation.

With the exception of a few opportune changes, the code repeats the older discipline in this matter. According to canon 6, nn. 2 and 3, therefore, the doctrine proposed is to be interpreted according to the old law and its commentators.

To understand what canonical institution is, one must have an understanding of what canonical provision in general signifies. In this the Code helps. "Canonical provision," according to the Code, "is understood the concession of an ecclesiastical office, made according to the norms of the sacred canons, by a ompetent ecclesiastial superior.[12] In other words, it is in general the canonical process by which one is put into the possession of a benefice. If the canonical provision follows upon the presentation of a patron, it is called *canonical institution.*

Canonical provision implies a three-fold act:

(a) The *designation of a person,* to be prefixed to an office.

10 X, *"De Institutionibus,"* III, 7.

11 Wernz II, 429 and 442.

12 C. 147, par. 2.

(b) The *concession of the title* or of the ecclesiastical office itself.

(c) The introduction to the actual possession of the office.[13]

The older canonists distinguished a three-fold institution:

(a) Institution collativa tituli; (b) Institutio corporalis; (c) Institutio authorizabilis. The first is defined by Wernz,[14] who bases his definition on the teaching of Lourin and Schmalzgrueber—The necessary concession of the title to an ecclesiastical office, at the instance of a patron presenting, or other privileged person nominating or presenting, the concession being made by the competent ecclesiastical superior. The *corporal institution* is the act of placing a cleric who already has the jus ad rem to an office, in the actual possession of that office. *Authorizable institution,* which according to Vermeersch is rare in our day, is not defined alike by the doctors. Wernz defines it: The approbation of the Bishop by which the cure of souls is committed to a cleric, once the cleric has received from an inferior Prelate promotion to a "curate" office by institution collativa tituli.

Authorizable institution is necessary only when, in case of a *curate* benefice, full provision (i.e., the authority to give the *jus in re,* or *institutio collativa tituli*) belongs to another than the Bishop, e.g., to a chapter. A S S XVII, 583; Aichner, 287.

Schmalzgrueber defines it: "Institutio clerico curato ad sacramenta administranda (facta) "ab Episcopo jure communi, vel ab aliis inferioribus vi privilegii apostolci, vel consuetudine saltem immemorabili" (III 7 de Institutionibus n. 40). Aichner: "Auctoritas data ab Episcopo in oves, seu commissio regendi."

13 Maroto I, 585.

14 Wernz II, 442.

Institution, in the canons under discussion, is "institutio collativa tituli"; in other words, that canonical process by which a cleric is given the "jus ad rem" to an ecclesiastical office or benefice.

Canon 1466

"One lawfully presented and found suitable, has the right, once he has accepted the presentation, to canonical institution.

"The right of granting canonical institution belongs to the Ordinary of the place, not to the Vicar General without a special mandate.

"If many or all those presented are found suitable, the Ordinary selects him whom he judges the more fit in the Lord."[15]

This canon repeats the old law "ex integro." For in the Decretals,[16] we read: "Si Episcopi post promotionem suam, praesentationes personarum ad ecclesias, a patronis earum, pro ecclesiis adepti fuerint; personae idoneae quas ad eas vacantes praesentaverint, sunt admittendae." This agrees with the first paragraph.

The doctrine of the second paragraph is directly from Trent,[17] which in turn was based on the Law of the Decretals. Trent decreed: "In casu autem fundationis, aut dotationis hujusmodi institutio Episcopo, et non alteri inferiori, reservetur." If, however, one inferior to the Bishop had lawfully obtained the right to institute, in virtue of special law; the examination as to fitness belonged, nevertheless, to the Ordinary of the place, according to the same Council of Trent: "Quod si ad inferiores institutio pertineat, ab Episcopo tamen, juxta alias statuta ab hac sancta synodo, examinentur: alioquin institutio ab inferioribus facta irrita sit et inanis."[18]

16 C. 18, X, *de jure patronatus*, III, 38; cf. Blat III, 370.
17 Sess. XIV, de ref., C. 12.
18 Sess. XXV, *de ref.*, C. 9.

According to the Sextus: "Officialis, aut vicarius generalis Episcopi beneficia conferre non possunt: nisi beneficiorum collatio ipsis specialiter sit commissa."[19]

The third paragraph comes from a chapter of Gregory IX's Decretals.[20] But whereas, in the chapter quoted, a distinction was made between the lay-patron and the ecclesiastical-patron, the new law, conformable with other canons of the new patronal legislation, omits this distinction, with the result that the present canon hold for presentees of both kinds of patrons. The chapter of the Decretals reads: "Quum advocatus (i.e., patron), clericum unum idoneum episcopo praesentaverit, et postulaverit postmodum, eo non refutato, alium aeque idoneum in eaden ecclesia admitti; quis eorum alteri praeferatur, judicio episcopo credimus relinquendum, si laicus fuerit, cui jus competit praesentandi."

The successive stages by which one comes into actual possession of an ecclesiastical benefice in case of presentation by a patron, are: first, the patron suggests the name of a candidate whom he thinks possesses the qualities necessary for the proper administration of the benefice, to the Ordinary of the place; secondly, the Ordinary declares the fitness of the candidate; thirdly, the Ordinary bestows on the candidate, whom he has approved the "jus ad rem" to the benefice. It is with this bestowal of the jus ad rem to the benefice, i.e., with "institutio collativa tituli," that the present canon deals.[21]

19 C. 3, *de officio Vicarii*, I, 13, in VI°.

20 C. 24, X, *de jure patronatus*, III, 38.

21 Par. 1. Missio in beneficii possessionem fiat secundum modum jure particulari praescriptum, vel legitima consuetudine receptum, nisi justa ex causa Ordinarius ab eo modo seu ritu expresse in scriptis dispensaverit; quo in casu haec dispensatio locum tenet captae possessionis," C. 1444, par. 1. Introduction into actual possession of a benefice is treated in canon 1444 of the Code, which says that the manner in which installation ("missio in possessionem") should take place is prescribed by particular—for instance, diocesan—statutes or by custom, which must be observed unless the Ordinary has granted a written dispensation from its observance. In this case the dispensation takes the place of formal installation. Cf. Augustine VI, p. 521.

Just as no one may present himself to a benefice, so no one may institute himself in a benefice. There must be a distinction between the one who confers and the one who receives. The reason of this distinction is not only to avoid the semblance of base ambition, but because the conferring of a benefice implies an exercise of spiritual power, which power is generally had only in the Ordinary of the place. The Ordinary has an "intentio in jure fundata" to confer all the benefices in his territory,[22] and therefore the intention "in jure fundatam" likewise to make provision which follows upon presentation, i.e., "institutio." Inferiors may thus provide only when they have special permission to do so. Superiors, below the Roman Pontiff, may provide, i.e., institute clerics only in cases where the Ordinary has been remiss in his duties.[23]

The appointment must have been accepted by the presentee before the Ordinary may licitly or validly make institution. This acceptance must be express. "Beneficium ecclesiasticum clerico invito et provisionem non expresse acceptanti valide conferri nequit."[24]

One change has been noted from the old law induced by the third paragraph of the canon under treatment; that is, that formerly only the lay patron had the right to vary his presentation,[25] and thus to present more than one candidate, whether simultaneously or successively, and that also the Ordinary could choose whom he wished only among those presented by lay patrons. But, since the *ecclesiastical* patron did not enjoy this right of varying his presentation, the Ordinary must appoint the candidate of the ecclesiastical patron, provided he was suitable. The Ordinary, in this case, had no choice between candidates unless several candidates were elected, and presented (cf. C. 153, Par. 2). This could

22 C. 1432, par. 1.

23 C. 274, n. 1.

24 C. 1436.

25 Cc. 5, 221, 29, X, *de jure patronatus*, III, 38; Ferraris IV v. *juspatronatus* nn. 55-58.

happen in the case of a patronage arising from two titles e.g., if the church or benefice was built by one moral person and endowed by another moral person. By the Code, both the lay and the ecclesiastical patron now enjoy the "jus variandi"[26] and, consequently, the Ordinary has the right to choose one among several presented. But there is another change which this paragraph seems to have introduced. The paragraph says that the Ordinary must select him whom he judges "magis idoneum." This seems to suggest that for all benefices subject to the right of presentation, the more fit, or more *worthy* person—as the old law expressed it—must be chosen by the Ordinary. Formerly this was not of obligation except for benefices involving the cure of souls. For, the Council of Trent had decreed: "Inferiora beneficia ecclesiastica, *praesertim* curam animarum habentia, personis dignis et habilibus. . . . conferantur."[27] "Digniores" were not demanded, according to the interpreters of the old law, except for beneficia curata.[28]

"Dignus censetur, in quo non desideratur ulla qualitas in beneficiato, spectata tam natura ipsius beneficii, quam fundatoris mente requisita. Unde *dignior* est, in quo qualitates illae excellunt, ut consideratis omnibus aptior esse judicetur ad obeundum officium annexum beneficio, cui est preferendus." Wiestner. I. c. n. 131.

It will aid to note here the principal qualities in virtue of which anyone, other things being equal, is thought "more worthy," and to be preferred to others in appointment to a benefice.

(1)—Qui est gremio ecclesiae praefertur alteri, qui non est de eodem gremio: indigena seu ordiundus—diocesanus—alenigenae et forensi, non diocesano. (Rule of the S. Chancery, 17.)

(2)—Praefertur ille de cujus bonis fundata est ecclesia. (C. 8 L XXI.)

26 C. 1460, par. 4.
27 Sess. VII, *de ref.*, c. 3.
28 Ferraris v. *beneficium*, art. V, nn. 28-30.

(3)—Doctor seu graduatus non doctori seu non graduato praefertur.

(4)—Senior juniori praefertur.

(5)—Praesens in curia absenti. (Rule 17 S. Chancery.)

(6)—Sacerdos non sacerdoti, etiamsi ad beneficium non curato.[29]

Canon 1467
Time Within Which Canonical Appointment Is to Be Made

"Canonical appointment to all benefices, even to those not involving the cure of souls, is to be made, if no just impediment stand in the way, within two months from the time presentation has been made."[30]

Before the Code, canonical appointment, or institution, had to be made within a reasonable time.[31] The comprehension of this reasonable time was not definitely determined, at least, not for all benefices. The constitution of Pius V, "In conferendis" of March 18, 1567, fixed the time for appointment to parochial benefices at two months.[32] For other offices, however, it was merely negatively determined that appointment should not be made until the patron had been given time to make presentation. Any appointment made prior to the presentation could be declared void, at the instance of the patron.[33]

The new legislation extends the former to all benefices. Thus the Code advisedly employs the expression, "etiam non curato." Wherefore, canonical institution to all benefices, whether having the cure of souls attached or not, must be made within two months.

The time is "tempus utile"; it admits delays. It is to be interpreted according to canon 34, par. 3, n. 1. The first day is not to be reckoned. Thus, if the presentation

29 Ferraris v. *beneficium*, art. V, nn. 44-64.

30 C. 1467.

31 Wernz II, 445.

32 Fontes Jur. Can., n. 119; Wernz II, 445.

33 C. 8, *de jure patronatus*, III, 38; Schmalzgrueber, III, 7, nn. 4, 24, 32.

were made on the third of January, canonical appointment ought to follow before or on the third of March.

Appointment may be made on any day, even on a ferial, and even outside the territory of the competent superior, for it is an act of voluntary jurisdiction, not of contentious jurisdiction attended with the solemnities and noise of a trial. This was the old discipline at least, which still holds after the Code, inasmuch as the new legislation is silent in the matter.[34]

In case of failure on the part of the Ordinary to make appointment within the time prescribed by the canon, the appointment devolves upon the Metropolitan.[35]

Canon 1468

Renunciation by or Death of Presentee Before Canonical Institution

"If a presentee renounces before canonical institution (his right to appointment), or dies, the patron has the right of presenting anew."[36]

The doctrine of this canon is likewise new in written law. It is a corollary of canon 1460, par. 4, which admits to all patrons the right of varying their presentation. And it is equitable, as Blat observes.[37]

"If the presentee," says Blat, in the same place, "whose fitness has not yet been declared, or even if he has been found fit, a) *before canonical appointment*, when *prima de jure vacatio perseverat*, renounces his right to canonical institution obtained by virtue of canon 1466; b) or dies, in both cases the patron, according to canon 1457, has the right of presenting anew."

By this, Blat would imply the Code repeats itself, when in canon 1465 it admits to the patron the right to vary his presentation and to present more than one candidate, either at the same time, or one after the other. Rather, it would seem that the canon has in view only

34 Wernz II, 445; Schmalzgrueber III, 7, n. 28.

35 C. 274, n. 1.

36 C. 1468, CIC.

37 Wernz II, 494-495; Blat III, 372.

the case where the renunciation is made *after the fitness of the candidate has been pronounced upon,* for only then would there be need of the present canon. This canon, evidently takes care only of the emergency when, after a candidate has been already declared fit, and has thus obtained a "jus quaesitum" to canonical appointment,[38] which is the effect of a presentation lawfully made renounces his right to institution; otherwise, since by the mere fact that one is presented, the presentee obtains no right of any kind until he has been declared suitable by the Ordinary, the renunciation spoken of in the canon would mean nothing, for there would be nothing to renounce.[39] The canon then means that if, after the presentee has been accepted by the Ordinary, and has obtained a right to receive canonical institution within the time prescribed by the law—two months from the day presentation is made, providing no just impediment stand in the way (can. 1467), renounces his right or dies. In the latter case, viz., in case of death, there is no difficulty, for then, the whole matter is in statu quo ante presentationem, and a new presentation is in order.

Though a corollary of canon 1465, the canons are not to be confused. Canon 1465 considers the case when an *unworthy* candidate has been presented. In this canon, to the contrary, there is a question of a worthy candidate, who has been accepted by the Ordinary, and who has obtained the right to canonical appointment. It is equitable that the patron be not deprived of his right to present simply because the candidate of his choice renounces his lawfully acquired right to receive appointment at the hands of the Ordinary. Since the deprivation of the right to present in this contingency would be in the nature of a punishment, and no one should be punished unless he be guilty of some misdemeanor, the equitableness of the canon is apparent.

38 C. 184 CIC; cf. Maroto I, 679.

39 C. 187, par. 2 CIC; cf. Maroto I, 682.

CHAPTER VIII

Canon 1469
THE DUTIES OF PATRONS

The Code reminds patrons in its definition of the "juspatronatus" that the right of patronage consists not merely of privileges, but likewise of corresponding duties. These duties are:

(1)—"To advise the Ordinary of the place, if the resources of the (Patronal) church or benefice have begun to fail, without, however, meddling in the administration of those resources.

(2)—"If the right of patronage which they enjoy has arisen from the title of building ('ex titulo aedificationis'), to build anew or repair a demolished church in such a manner as the Ordinary deems necessary—except, however, when the burden of building anew or repairing the church devolves upon others according to canon 1186.

(3)—"If the right of patronage is held by the title of endowment ('ex titulo dotationis'), the duty of supplying funds adequate to a decent maintenance of the church or benefice, when these lack sufficient resources."[1]

The first number of this paragraph of the canon is based upon the doctrine of the 9th Council of Toledo,[2] which decreed that patrons advise the local Ordinary, if the resources of the church or benefice of their patronage begin to fail (dilapidari), "without, however, mixing themselves in the administration of those resources." This canon of the Toledo Council was thus evolved by Trent. But the patrons of benefices, of whatsoever order or dignity they be, be they even communities, universities, or any college whatsoever, whether of clerics or lay-

1 C. 1469.

2 C. I, Conc. Tolet. IX (a. 655)—Labbe & Cossart VI, 452; cf. c. 31, C. XVI, qu. VII.

men, shall not in any way, nor for any manner of cause or occasion, meddle with the receiving of the fruits, rents or revenues of any benefice whatsoever, even though those benefices be truly, by foundation or endowment, under their right of patronage; but shall leave them to the free disposal of the rector, or of the beneficiary, any custom to the contrary notwithstanding."[3] A fortiori, the above exclusion is to be understood concerning the administration of spiritual things and concerning inspection of church goods and visitation of the ornaments of the patronal church, as the notes to this part of the canon indicate. "As regards patrons," says the Tridentine synod in another chapter of the same title, "they shall not presume in any way to interfere in those things which regard the administration of the sacraments; neither shall they meddle in the visitation of the ornaments of the church, or its revenues arising from landed property, or from buildings, except in so far as they are competent to do so by the institution or foundation."[4]

Thus, the beneficiary or rector of the patronal church or benefice is by law the administrator of both the spiritual and temporal affairs of benefices.[5] By privilege, however, as is insinuated by the decree of Trent just cited, some patrons—especially lay patrons may have a share in the administration of the temporalities of the patronal benefice.[6] But these privileges must be proved to exist before they can be admitted, since the presumption of the law is against them.

Number 2 of the paragraph under discussion comes to us from the Council of Trent. There, speaking of the obligation of Bishops to provide for the restoration and repair of demolished churches, the Council says: "As regards parish-churches which have thus (i.e., through the injury of time) fallen into decay, they (the Bishops)

3 Sess. XXV, de ref., C. 9.

4 Sess. XXIV, de ref., C. 3.

5 Cf. C. 1472.

6 Cf. 1475, par. 1; Blat III, 380.

shall, even though they be under the right of patronage, make it their care that they be repaired and restored, out of any fruits and proceeds whatsoever, in any way belonging to said churches; and if those resources should not be sufficient, they shall compel by all suitable means, the patrons and others who receive any fruits from these churches, or, in their default, the parishoners, to provide for the aforesaid repairs, setting aside every appeal, exemption, or reservation whatsoever."[7]

According to the New Law, this duty of the patron is conditional, viz., if the patron wish to retain his right of patronage.[8] Wherefore, if the patron refuse to repair or rebuild, as the case may demand, no judicial action may be brought about to compel him to do so. But a time may be fixed by the Ordinary, or by the common law, within which the obligation is to be performed, or the right of patronage renounced. By the New Law, the time is left to the judgment of the Ordinary; if not complied with, the right of patronage ipso jure ceases.[9]

We are to observe in the canon that the duty of repairing or rebuilding is not common to all patrons, but peculiar to those who possess the patronal right "ex titulo aedificationis," that is, in virtue of having built the patronal church or benefice. Nor is the obligation absolute for them. It may fall on others first. Canon 1186 is to be considered in the matter. This canon, speaking of the duty of repairing a parochial church, says in its second paragraph: Salvis peculiaribus legitimisque consuetudinibus et conventionibus, et firma obligatione quae ad aliquem spectet etiam ex constituto legis civilis: 2—Onus reficiendi ecclesiam paroecialem incumbit ordine qui sequitur:

Bonis fabricae ecclesiae, ut supra (in paragraph 1); Patrono.

7 Sess. XXV, de ref., C. 7.

8 Cf. C. 1451; 1469, par. 3; cf. Coronata, par. 65.

9 C. 1469, par. 3.

Thus, the duty of repairing a parochial church is incumbent, first, upon the fabric of the church (i.e., the revenues of the church, in general); secondly, upon the patron.

But lawful customs, concordats, exemptions, and even the civil law—of certain places, such as Austria, Poland, etc.—are to be taken into account. These may place the obligation upon the patron first of all. Or, they may exempt the patron entirely. The particular laws of different countries remain unchanged, and are to be observed.[10]

If the patron possess a rescript of exemption, or if the bill of foundation exempt him, the patron is not bound to this duty, at least as regards parochial churches.

As long as the patronal church stands in need of *necessary* repairs, that is, of those repairs which are required for the carrying on of the divine worship, the right of patronage remains suspended.[11]

The third number of the paragraph is likewise founded upon the Tridentine discipline. It rests upon the principle: "Ubi est emolumentum, ibi debet esse onus." The chapter of Trent in question has been given in the former number of the canon; here it will be necessary only to remark that the chapter quoted imposed the duty of repairing the church on "all" patrons, no matter from what title their right of patronage has originated.[12]

The canon here refers only to those whose right of patronage has arisen from the title of endowment.[13] Such patrons must supply funds necessary for the decent support of the pastor, or beneficiary, and for the decent maintenance of divine worship, "whether these (funds) remain from the original foundation, or have suffered diminution on account of the circumstances of time and place."

10 Coronata, paragraphs 63, 64
11 C. 1469, par. 2.
12 Sess. XXI, *de ref.*, C. 7.
13 C. 1469, par. 1, n. 3.

Paragraph two says:[14] "If the church has collapsed or needs necessary repairs, or the revenues have failed according to the norm of numbers 2 and 3 of the first paragraph of the canon, the right of patronage meanwhile may not be exercised."

Paragraph three has:[15] "If the patron, within the time fixed by the Ordinary under penalty of cessation of the right of patronage, has rebuilt or restored, or increased the revenues of the church, his right of patronage revives: otherwise, it ceases *ipso jure* and without any express declaration to that effect."

These two paragraphs regard the *suspension* of the right of patronage in the event that the patronal church or benefice, which have become unfit for the celebration of divine services, are not restored in a manner deemed sufficient by the Ordinary for the conduct of liturgical functions.

These paragraphs must not be confounded with the next canon, which treats of the *suppression* and *cessation* of the right of patronage;[16] here there is question only of the *suspension* of the patronal right.

Paragraph two would seem to include rights of patronage which have arisen from any title—whether *original* or *derived,* e.g., *venditionis, emptionis,* etc., whereas paragraph one mentions explicitly only those patronages which have arisen from the title of "building" and "dowry," for paragraph two makes no distinction.[17] Furthermore, the exercise of the right of patronage over a church or benefice unfit for use would be useless. Although, therefore, those patrons who enjoy the *juspatronatus* from a "derived" title are not obliged by the first paragraph of the canon to rebuild or re-endow dilapidated or bankrupt churches, practically, their lot is no better than that of those upon whom rests the obliga-

14 C. 1469, par. 2.
15 C. 1469, par. 3.
16 C. 1470, par. 1.
17 Cf. Blat III, 373.

tion of rebuilding or re-endowing, for neither the one nor the other may lawfully exercise the right of patronage as long as the church or benefice remains thus.[18] But inasmuch as the right of the latter does not revive unless the condition of the patronal church or benefice is bettered *by themselves*, the right of the former does revive, no matter by whom the church or benefice has been restored to its pristine condition—that is, whether they have been restored by themselves or by others.[19]

The permission granted to the Ordinary in the third paragraph, viz., to determine the time within which the patronal church or benefice must be restored under penalty of the cessation of the right of patronage is based upon the 25th Regula Juris: "Mora sua cuilibet est niciva."[20] This rule, however, must be properly interpreted. "Tempus utile," which admits lawful interruptions, is granted by the canon. Wherefore, if one has lawful reasons for being excused from the exact observance of the time fixed by the Ordinary, the Ordinary must take this into account. "Non enim est in mora, qui potest exceptione legitima se tueri."[21] Prudence will be the Ordinary's guide. And since there is here the question of a penalty, the patron should be favored in cases of doubt.[22] If, however, the "tempus utile" has elapsed, and the patron has not complied with the Ordinary's command, the right of patronage *ipso jure*, without any express declaration, ceases.

18 C. 1469, paragraphs 2, 3.

19 C. 1469, par. 3: "Secus ipso jure et sine ulla declaratione cessat."

20 C. 25, R. 1, in VI°.

21 C. 60, R. I, in VI°.

22 C. 2214, par. 2.

CHAPTER IX

Canon 1470

How the Right of Patronage Is Extinguished

It has been seen in the preceding canon that if the patron does not build anew, or repair, or re-endow, a church which has been destroyed, demolished, or bankrupt, respectively, within the time prescribed by the Ordinary under penalty of cessation of the right of patronage, *by law*, without any express declaration, ceases.[1]

Besides this case, there are many other ways in which the right of patronage ceases.

Thus, if a patron renounce his right of patronage, his right ceases.[2] He may renounce his right of patronage entirely, i.e., the whole sum of the privileges granted him in canon 1455, or simply the right of presentation, as the Legislator wishes in canon 1451, par. 1, or the honorary privileges granted him either by general or particular law, as e.g., his right to a seat of honor in his patronal church, or the privilege of having his family coat-of-arms hung up in the church or benefice of his patronage.[3] He may not, however, renounce a right of patronage which he possesses in collegio with other patrons, if from his renunciation any damage would accrue to the other patrons.[4]

Since the right of patronage is in the nature of a privilege, renunciation follows the laws by which a priv-

1 C. 1469, par. 3.

2 " . . . juspatronatus extinguitur; I°—Si patronus juri suo renuntiaverit; ejus tamen renuntiatio ex integro fieri potest aut ex parte; nunquam vero potest aliis compatronis, si qui sint, damnum afferre." C. 1470, par. 1, n. 1; cf. 272, par. 2.

3 Cf. Blat III, 374.

4 R. I. 29 in VI°; "Quod omnes tangit debet ab omnibus approbari"; et 33 ibid: "Mutare consilium quis non potest in alterius detrimentum."

ilege may be renounced. Thus, the renunciation must be made, either verbally or in writing, to the competent ecclesiastical superior. A privilege granted to a private person, e.g., a personal right of patronage, may be lawfully renounced, since it is given in favor of the person himself. Private persons may not renounce a privilege granted in favor of a whole community, to a place, or to the person because of the dignity which he has.[5]

Secondly, the right of patronage is extinguished if the Holy See revokes it, or suppresses in perpetuum the church or benefice to which the right of patronage is attached.[6] For we have seen that as regards its stability, the right of patronage is a jus quaesitum, which can lawfully be revoked by the Supreme Pontiff. From the first Regula Juris we know that "Omnis res per quascumque causas nascitur, per easdem dissolvitur."[7] The right of patronage is "from the concession of the Church.[8] Since, too, for the existence of a right, an object in which the right inheres is necessary, if the object is wanting, the right too ceases.[9]

Thirdly, the right of patronage ceases by prescription, i.e., if during the time prescribed by the civil laws of various nations (which the Canon Law follows in regard to prescription), no exercise of the right of patronage has been made, or if during the whole time the Ordinary has collated freely to the church or benefice in question. In following the civil law in the matter of prescription the Code settles many disputes formerly had among the doctors concerning the time within which prescription has the force of law.[10]

5 C. 72, par. 3, 4.

6 " . . . jus patronatus extinguitur—Si Sancta Sedes jus patronatus revocaverit aut ipsam ecclesiam vel beneficium perpetuo suppresserit," C. 1470, par. 1, n. 2; cf. C. 1422.

7 R. I. in V I°—1.

8 C. 1448.

9 Cf. Wernz, I, 45; Aichner, pp. 1 and 2 and par. 94.

10 C. C. 1508 seq.; cf. Wernz II, 438; Aichner, par. 94; Blat III, 374.

Fourthly, the right of patronage is extinguished, if the thing (church or benefice) to which the right of patronage is attached perishes. Or if the family or gens or line to which, according to the bill of foundation, it is reserved, is extinguished. In the latter case, the right of patronage does not become hereditary, i.e., does not pass on to the heirs of the founder—whether they be heirs by will, or intestate heirs, or whatsoever other kind, nor can the Ordinary *validly* permit the right of patronage in this case to be donated to another.[11]

This paragraph of the canon refers in its first phrase to the real juspatronatus, which may be according to the bill of foundation, indult, etc., familiare, gentilitium or mixed. If the thing to which such right of patronage attaches perishes, since the right lacks an object in which it resides, it is extinguished; or if the family, tribe or clan, or hereditary line which alone can validly exercise the right is extingushed; since the right would then lack a lawful subject who may exercise it, the right itself is extinguished.

In this connection, we are referred by Blat to a chapter of the Sextus of Boniface VIII, which says: "Si laicus jus patronatus Ecclesiae sibi competens eidem, vel alteri ecclesiae, vel loco religioso duxerit conferendum hujusmodi collatio quamvis absque consensu Episcopi facta fuerit, efficax est censenda. Per praefatam tamen collationem juri Episcopi qui eidem assensum non praebuit, nolumus in aliquo derogari."[12]

From this chapter Blat concludes[13] that a lay patron may, with the Bishop's consent, give, viz., by donation, his right of patronage to a church, monastery, pious

11 " . . . juspatronatus extinguitur: Si res, sui jus patronatus inhaeret, pereat, aut extinguatur familia, gens, linea cui secundum tabulas fundationis reservatur; quo in altero casu nec jus patronatus hereditarium evadit, nec Ordinarius valide permittere poterit donationem juris patronatus alii fieri," C. 1470, par. 1, n. 4.

12 C. un *de jurepatronatus*, III, 19 in VI°.

13 Blat III, 374.

place, etc. But he may not give it to a private person, because in doing so he would implicitly renounce his right, and then proceed to give that right, which he would not then possess, to another. In this we do not agree with Blat, even though at the time the donation was made it was not explicitly foreseen that the family, gens, or hereditary line was extinguished. For first, the canon says "alii," and does not distinguish, whether that "other" is a physical or a moral person; therefore, we should not distinguish. Secondly, the canons of this chapter are to be interpreted strictly; therefore, the "other" should be made to include both physical and moral persons. We conclude, therefore, that in case the family, etc., to whom the right of patronage belongs is extinguished, the right cannot be lawfully given over either to a private person, nor to a moral person, such as a religious place, to a monastery, to another church, or to any other moral person whatsoever.

Fifthly, the right of patronage is extinguished, if with the consent of the patron, the patronal church or benefice is united to a church or benefice of free collation, or if the church or benefice subject to the right of patronage becomes *elective or regular.*[14]

According to canon 1424, Ordinaries cannot lawfully unite a benefice subject to the right of patronage with a benefice of free collation without the patron's consent. The reason of this is that the law-giver wishes to protect the lawfully acquired rights of all.[15] Although it be true that the Code is not any too lovingly inclined towards the right of patronage, as Vermeesch observes,[16] it does not wish that that by the union of benefices, the patron's right be molested. For, according to canon 1420, by an "unio extinctiva" the right of patronage would be extinguished, by an "unio aeque principalis,"

14 " . . . jus patronatus extinguitur: Si, consentiente patrono, ecclesia vel beneficium uniatur alii liberae collationis, aut ecclecia fiat electiva vel regularis," C. 1470, par. 1, n. 5.

15 C. 4, C. I. C.

16 Vermeersch II, 776 and 781.

of two benefices, one of which is patronal benefice, the right of the benefice of free collation would be injured. Therefore, the consent of the patron is necessary in order that the right of patronage be extinguished.

A church or benefice becomes elective when it falls under the administration of a chapter of canons; *regular* when it comes into possession of a body of exempt religious.[17]

That the right of patronage be extinguished in any of the three cases noted in this number of the canon, it is necessary that the consent of the patron, either oral or written, but preferably written because of its greater probatory character, be given. This consent is ad validitatem.[18]

Sixthly, the right of patronage is extinguished if the patron has attempted to transfer his right of patronage simoniacally to another; if he has lapsed into apostasy, heresy or schism; if he has unjustly usurped or unjustly kept in his possession the goods or rights of the patronal church or benefice; if he has killed or mutilated, either by himself or by others, the rector or other cleric given over to the service of the church, or the beneficiary himself.[19]

A *declaratory* sentence suffices and is required in order that patrons be thought to have lost their right of patronage because of the crimes mentioned in the above paragraph.[20]

In the case of the crime mentioned in the last phrase

17 Blat III, 374; cf. C. 25, X, *de jurepatronatus*, III, 38; "Ceterum conventualis ecclesia, non electioni praelati faciendae, sed jam factae honestius patroni postulatur assensus; nisi aliter de sua jurisdictione obtineat, ut partes suas interponere debeat electioni tractandae."

18 C. 1424; Blat 374, 5°; cf. Reiffenstuehl, III, 38, *De Jure Patronatus* n. 125.

19 C. 1470, par. 1, n. 6; " . . . jus patronatus extinguitur; Si patronus jus patronatus simoniace in alium transferre attentaverit; si lapsus fuerit in apostasiam, heresim aut schisma; si bona ac jura ecclesiae vel beneficii injuste usurpaverit aut detineat: si rectorum vel alium clericum ecclesiae servitio addictum aut beneficiarium per se vel per alios occiderit vel mutilaverit."

20 C. 1470, par. 3.

of the paragraph, viz., the killing or grave injury of the rector, beneficiary, etc., the penalty of extinction of the right of patronage extends likewise to the heirs of the patron, if the right be an hereditary right of patronage.[21]

The above number of this canon requires a more or less lengthy explanation.

If a patron, whether lay or ecclesiastical, *attempts* to transfer his right of patronage, whether this right be personal or real, simoniacally, his right of patronage is thereby extinguished. The word "attentaverit" of the canon is used advisedly, for a simoniacal contract is ipso jure invalid, according to canon 729, and canonical provision made subsequently is without any juridical effect. We have seen that the juspatronatus is a "jus spirituali annexum," and thus liable to simoniacal abuse. Already had been declared by Alexander III.,[22] "Cum inconveniens sit vendi jus patronatus quod est spirituali annexum; contractum illum irritum esse decernimus." And the Council of Trent: Nec dictum jus patronatus, venditionis, aut alio quocumque titulo, in alios contra canonicas sanctiones transferre praesumant patroni; si secus fecerint, excommunicationis et interdicti poenis subjiciantur et dicto jure patronatus ipso jure privati existant."[23] Before the Code, the penalty of excommunication or interdict was ferendae sententiae,[24] now it is determined by the law itself, i.e., latae sententiae.[25]

21 C. 1470, par. 2.

22 C. 16, X, de jurepatronatus, III, 38.

23 Sess. XXV, *de ref*, C. 9.

24 "Si secus fecerint, excommunicationis et interdicti poenis subjiciantur" of Sess. XXV, *de ref*, C. 9, just cited. Cf. Blat III, 374.

25 C. 2392, nn. 1-3: "Firmo praescripto can. 729, delictum perpetrantes simoniae in quibuslibet officiis, beneficiis aut dignitatibus ecclesiasticis:

1° Incurrunt in excommunicationem latae sententiae Sedi Apostolicae simpliciter reservatam:

2° Ipso facto privati in perpetuum monent jure eligendi, praesentandi nominandi, si quod habeant.

3° Si clerici sint, praeterea suspendantur" (i.e., ferendae sententiae).

Furthermore, according to the New Law, clerics are to be suspended, ferendae sententiae.

In this matter, the general rules concerning simony apply. It may be either simony of divine right or simony of ecclesiastical right, according to the definitions of these given in canon 727. Furthermore, the simony comprised under the penalty laid down in canon 2392, is not only simonia realis, but likewise simonia conventialis,[26] according to the definition of canon 728; "Emptiovenditio, permutatio, etc., late accipienda sunt pro qualibet conventione *licet ad effectum non deducta.*" And under the term simonia conventionalis, we must include in this matter the simonia *confidentialis*, which is, according to Schmalzgrueber,[27] a kind of simonia conventionalis, "qua quis beneficium ecclesiasticum alicui quocumque modo v.g., eligendo, presentando, conferendo, vel in ejus favorem resignando, procurat com expresso vel tacito pacto, ut is, cui id procurat, post aliquod idem beneficium ipsi procuranti vel alteri resignet, aut pensionem vel fructus ex eo praestet."

The simony must be proved, and a declaratory sentence given as remarked above, in order that the right of patronage become extinguished.

The apostasy, heresy, and schism, spoken of in the second phrase of this number of the canon, are to be accepted in the sense of canon 1325, par. 2. Thus an apostate is one who, after the reception of baptism, retaining the name of being a Christian, pertinaciously denies, or doubts any of the truths to be believed either "fide divina or fide ecclesiastica"; a heretic, one who recedes entirely from the Christian faith; a schismatic, one who rejects to subject himself to the Supreme Pontiff, or who refuses to be in communion with the members of the Church who are subject to the Supreme Pontiff. If the patron, therefore, become an apostate, a heretic

26 Eichmann, "Strafrecht," par. 100, pp. 222, seq.

27 Schmalzgrueber V, III, n. 37: cf. Eichmann, as above.

or a schismatic, and is declared so by a declaratory sentence, his right of patronage is extinguished.

The next phrase of the paragraph which we are considering says that if the patron has *unjustly* usurped or unjustly retains the *goods* or *rights* of the church or benefice, his right of patronage is extinguished after a declaratory sentence of the competent judge.

This unjust usurpation and retention can happen in various ways. First, by presentation to a benefice not juridically vacant; by presentation of one who already possesses a benefice; by putting a presentee into a benefice without canonical institution; by unduly meddling in the administration of the patronal church, etc.[28]

The doctrine herein contained comes from the Council of Trent, which declared: "Si quem clericorum vel laicorum, quacumque is dignitate . . . praefulgeat, in tantum malorum omnium radix cupiditatis occupaverit, ut alicujus ecclesiae, seu cujusvis saecularis vel regularis beneficii...jurisdictiones, bona, census, ac jura, etiam feudalia et emphyteutica, fructus, emolumenta, seu quacumque obventione, quae in ministrorum et pauperum necessitates converti debent; per se vel alios vi, vel timore incusso, seu etiam per suppositas personas clericorum aut laicorum, seu quacumque arte, aut quocumque quaesito colore, in proprios usus convertere, illosque usurpare praesumpserit, seu (this does not seem to be comprehended under the canon in question) impedire, ne ab iis, ad quos jure pertinent, percipiantur; is, . . . si ejus dem ecclesiae patronus fuerit, etiam jure patronatus, ultra praedictas poenas, eo ipso privatus existat."[29]

The fourth and last case considered in No. 6 of paragraph one of this canon is when the patron kills or gravely injures the rector or beneficiary, or other cleric given over to the service of the church or benefice of patronage, whether the killing or injury are made either

28 Blat III, 374.
29 Sess. XXII, *de ref*, C. 11.

by the patron himself or at the instigation of the patron, by another.

This doctrine is taken from the law of the Decretals.[30] In the place referred to, Innocent III says: "Sacri nihilominus Concilii approbatione statuimus quatenus si patroni . . . alicujus ecclesiae, rectorem vel clericum alium ejusdem ecclesiae, per se vel per alios occidere, vel mutilare ausu nefando praesumpserint, patroni jus patronatus. . prorsus ammittant. Et ne minus vindictae, quam memoria prorogetur . . . de praemissis nihil perveniat ad heredes."[31]

A cleric is understood one who has received at least tonsure.[32] And in this case, the cleric must have been attached to the patronal church or benefice with "aliqua saltem permamentia."[33]

Paragraph 2 of the canon notes that in case of the crimes mentioned in number 6 of the first paragraph (just explained), only the patron who has committed the crimes mentioned is deprived of the right of patronage, with the exception of the crime last spoken, viz., in case of the crime of killing or seriously injuring the beneficiary, etc., in which case, the privation of the right of patronage extends also to his heirs.

By the very fact of commission of the crimes mentioned in par. 1, No. 6, the right of patronage is not extinguished. A declaratory sentence,[34] i.e., a sentence of the competent judge, viz., ratione rei sitae,[35] is required and is sufficient. The declaratory sentence

30 C. 12, X, *de poenis* V 37.

31 You will note the derogation of this chapter of the Decretals effected by the New Law. The Decretals said: "De praemissis nihil perveniat ad heredes"; the Code: "Propter crimina de quibus in paragraph 1, n. 6, jus patronatus amittit solus patronus reus, et ob delictum postremo memoratum (i.e., in the case of killing or serious injury to beneficiary, etc., by the patron) *ejus quoque haeredes.*" C. 1470, paragraph 2.

32 C. 108, paragraph 1.

33 Blat III, 374.

34 C. 1470, par. 3.

35 C. 1560, n. 2; C. 1564.

merely states that the penalty latae sententiae has been incurred by the commission of the crime for which it is inflicted.[36] The declaration carries the penalty back to the time that the crime was committed, i.e., it has retroactive force.[37] Unless, however, the crime has been notorious, any acts, v.g., presentation, made before the declaratory sentence has been given, are valid.[38]

The fourth paragraph of the canon declares that those branded by censure or infamy of law, after a declaratory or condemnatory sentence, cannot, as long as the censure or infamy last, exercise the right of patronage, or enjoy the privileges of patronage.[39]

The censure may be excommunication, suspension, or interdict; the infamy, of any of those cases expressed in the common law,[40] e.g., perjurors, simulators of the Sacraments, public blasphemers.[41] Such persons may not exercise the right of presentation, have their family or tribal coat-of-arms in their patronal church, or any of the other privileges of patrons given by common or particular law, until they have been absolved from the censure or infamy.[42]

But such persons do not lose the right of patronage itself; they are prohibited only from its use and privileges.[43]

36 Eichmann, "Strafrecht," par. 12, p. 69.

37 Eichmann, "Strafrecht," par. 12, p. 69.

38 C. 2232, par. 1; "Poena latae sententiae, sive medicinalis sive vindicativa qui delicti sibi sit conscius, ipso facto in utroque foro tenet; ante sententiam tamen declaratoriam a poena observanda delinquens excusatur quoties eam servare sine infamia nequit, et in foro exteruo ab eo ejusdem poenae observantiam erigere nemo potest, nisi delictum sit notorium, firmo praescripto ca. 2223, par. 4." Cf. Eichmann, "Strafrecht," par. 12, p. 69.

39 C. 1470, par. 4. "Censura aut infamia juris innodati post sententiam condemnatoriam vel declaratoriam, usque dum censura vel infamia perdurant, nequeunt jus patronatus exercere ejusque privilegiis uti."

40 C. 2255, par. 1; C. 2293, par. 2.

41 Cf. CC. 2320-2329.

42 Although, as Blat observes, it is not necessary to take down the pastoral coat-of-arms, especially, we think, since they are usually stability fixed in the church and could not be removed without doing harm to the church. Cf. Blat III, 374.

43 C. 1470, par. 4.

CHAPTER X

Canon 1471

Distinction Between Right of Patronage and Presentation

In the last canon of the chapter on the right of patronage the code makes a very welcome observation. It tells us the right of patronage and the right of presentation are not synomymous terms in canon law. There is a well-defined distinction between them.[44] Not every right of presentation may be considered a right of presentation may be considered a right of patronage, and vice versa. The canon says:

"If the Holy See, either in concordats, or outside of concordats by indult, has granted to anyone the right of *presenting* to a vacant church or benefice, there does not arise from that concession the right of patronage, and the right of presentation is to be interpreted strictly according to the tenor of the indult."[45]

This canon, says Blat,[46] supposes that the right of presentation is enjoyed by persons who are not patrons. It also implies that there are some persons, moral or physical, who possess the right of patronage and yet may not present to vacancies. Who these persons are cannot be determined except in a most general manner. Negatively, one may state that those who enjoy the right of

44 "Praesentatio est jus designandi et offerendi clericum idoneum ab Episcopo vel competente Praelato in officio ecclesiastico vacante necessario in instituendum," Wernz II, 424 L, "Jus patronatus est summa privilegiorum, etc." CC. 1448, 1455.

45 C. 1471.

46 Blat III, 375.

presentation in virtue of concordats are usually rulers.[47] And those who enjoy the right of presentation in virtue of indult are as a rule extraordinary benefactors. In every case, the concordat or indult is to be examined and subjected to a strict interpretation, so far as the right of presentation is concerned.

It has been seen in the definition of patronage that the juspatronatus is a *sum* of privileges. It consists usually of the right of presentation, of the right of sustenance in case of need, and of certain honorary privileges. If one possess merely the right of presentation, without the right to sustenance in case of need, his right is properly designated a "right of presentation"; only by an unlawful extension of the term may he be said to possess the right of patronage. If, however, one possess the right to sustenance and the other honorary rights enumerated in canon 1455, without the right of presentation, his right may very properly be styled a right of patronage, despite the fact that he may not present to the church or benefice of his foundation.[48]

The canon would seem to indicate that the only reason why the legislator does not abrogate entirely the right of patronage is that he would provide for the emergency, which only too often arises[49] where the patron, or his heirs, suffer a change of fortune and become reduced to

47 Cf. Vermeersch II, 779. By the later Concordats the rulers of the following countries have the right of presentation over various ecclesiastical offices and benefices:

(a) Of Bavaria, Conc. of 1817, art. 9-11, *Raccolta* 594-595.
(b) Of Austria, Conc. of 1855, art. 19, Raccolta 825.
(c) Of France, Conc. of 1801, art. 4, 5, 16, 17, Raccolta 562-564.
(d) Of Spain, Conc. of 1851, art. 18, Raccolta 779-780.
(e) Of Portgual, Conc. of 1778, Art. I, Raccolta 509-511.
(f) Of the Catholic states of Central and South America, Costa Rica, Guatamala, Honduras, Nicaraugua, San Salvador, Venezuela, Equador, Columbia, etc., Raccolta di Concordati; 800, 810, 936, 948, 960, 971, 983, 1079, 1051 respectively; cf. Saegmueller, 255-258.

48 Such a juspatronatus the Code wishes from Canon 1451.

49 Cf. Pallotini, vol. XV, v. *patronus*, par 1.

material straits. For, in granting only the right of presentation to rulers in concordats, and not the right of sustenance, the Code insinuates that such concessions lack the usual foundations on which the benefactions of other patrons are based. For, very often, if not always, the presentations of rulers are acquired by usurpation, which the Church, to maintain peace, tolerates.[50] Those acquired by indult sometimes have a similar foundation,[51] though in singular cases the indult rests on more honorable grounds. In these latter instances, the right to sustenance and the other honorary privileges are not granted either because the benefactors do not need assistance, or simply because the Holy See did not deem it advisable to grant them.

From the fact that the canon makes explicit mention of concordats and Apostolic indults, in which the right of presentation is granted, we may conclude with reason, that if persons vindicate to themselves the right of patronage in virtue of other grants, e.g., by a bill of foundation, prescription, etc., and there is doubt whether merely the right of presentation was thereby granted, or the right of patronage strictly so-called, the presumption of the law is in favor of a right of patronage strictly so-called, with due respect, however, to canon 50, which we have already explained.[52]

Another point to be noticed in the canon under discussion is the obvious change made from the old law, "Beneficia principum sunt interpretanda largissime."[53] The "beneficium" of the right of patronage is not to be interpreted "largissime," according to the canon: to the contrary "Strictam interpretationem pati oportet."[54]

50 Saegmueller, pp. 280-282; pp. 285-287; Archiv. 61, 372; 78, 56.

51 Saegmueller, p. 281; Archiv. 61, 372; 78, 56.

52 In chapter on C. 1450.

53 C. 16, X, *de verborum significatione*, V 40.

54 C. 1471.

Some recent decisions of the S. Congregations of the Council give rise to a question concerning C. 1471, which may be discussed in conclusion of this study.

In three individual instances,[55] the Congregation has declared rights of presentation (the principal but "odious" part of the right of patronage), *over cathedral and collegiate churches,* which have not arisen from foundation or endowment, abolished by the Code, in virtue of C. 403. In the *"synopsis disceptionis,"* which, according to the custom of the Roman congregations, gives the general principles on which their decision is based, C. 1471 is cited in affirmation of their decisons. At first reading, the Congregation would appear to state that in view of the wording of this canon and that of C. 1448, the Code has abolished *all* rights of patronage and presentation which have not arisen from the foundation or endowment of a church or benefice.

The question, then naturally arises: Has the Code abolished all rights of patronage and presentation not based on foundation or endowment: or has it abrogated merely the rights of patronage and presentation over *cathedral and collegiate churches* not thus acquired?

If one considers the definition of patronage, in C. 1448, it is evident that the *juspatronatus* is recognized only to "founders." It would, therefore, exclude patrons by privilege and custom.[56] But against this canon, it may be urged that a definition is not a law; that, furthermore, if it be a law—dato sed non concesso—it refers only to future rights of patronage, for according to C. 10: "Leges respiciunt futura, non praeterita, nisi nominatim in eis de praeteritis caveatur"; in other words, the laws of the Code refer to the future not to the past—"Lex non habet oculos retro." In answer to this objection—apart from the fact that definitions in the Code describe things

55 S. Cong. Conc—Barul.—12 Nov., 1921, and 10 Jun., 1922, in A. A. S. XIV, 459-467; S. Cong. Conc. Utin. 19 Feb., 1921, in A. A. S. XIV, 551-554; S. Cong. Conc. Utinen. 10 Feb., 1923, in A. A. S. XV, 544-549.

56 Cf. S. Cong. Conc. in A. A. S. XIV, 464.

as they are, not as they will be in future—it is evident from C. 1450, paragraph 1, that no rights of patronage can be set up anew after the Code: the definition, therefore, plainly refers to those already existing.

Secondly, a strict interpretation, i.e., the interpretation favoring the liberty of the Church in making canonical provision—must be given to all the canons regarding the *jus patronatus*.[57] This is evident from the mind of the Legislator, and is confirmed on the authority of the Congregation of the Council.

Thirdly, the fact that the Council of Trent[58] explicitly abolished rights of patronage and presentation arising from custom and privilege—in other words, all rights of patronage (and presentation) not based on the title of foundation or endowment—would argue their abrogation also by Code, inasmuch as the mind of the new law is more firmly set against the *juspatronatus* than was Trent, as is evident from C. 1450, par. 1.

Despite these facts, however, it is not beyond all doubt, either from C. 1448, which does not expressly, abrogate such patronages, nor from C. 1471—which merely limits the *juspatronatus* granted by indults and concordats to a simple right of presentation—that the Code has abolished *all* rights of patronage and presentation which have not arisen from foundation or endowment.

So much is certain, viz., that rights of patronage and presentation *over cathedral and collegiate churches* are abolished by the Code, unless those rights have arisen from foundation or endowment. But this is in virtue of C. 403, which declares: "Dignities excepted, to the Bishops belong after hearing the chapter—(the right) to confer all and singly benefices and canonicates both in cathedral and in collegiate churches, every contrary custom being reprobated, and every contrary privilege revoked, the law of foundation, however, and the pre-

57 S. Cong. Conc. in A. A. S., XII, 164.
58 Sess. 24, *de ref*, c. 12.

scription of C. 1453, remaining in force," not, therefore, by virtue of CC. 1448 and 1471. Neither did the Congregation declare in those cases just cited rights of patronage and presentation abolished by CC. 1448 and 1471, but expressly because of C. 403.

The mind of the Legislator is doubtful as to rights of patronage and presentation over other churches and benefices. It is not evident from the Code that such rights have been abolished, even though they have not been acquired by foundation or endowment. The doubt is a *dubium juris*. Canon 15, therefore, would seem to apply: "Leges, etiam irritantes et inhabilitantes in dubio juris non urgent——"

In practice, therefore, what? It would seem that they may be exercised. For, until an authentic declaration removing the doubt is made by Rome, such patrons may enjoy their lawfully "acquired rights." In cases of controversy the norm of Canon 1458, par. 2, shall be observed. "Si vero his, quae intra utile tempus dirimi nequeat, exoriatur sive circa jus praesentandi inter Ordinarium et patronum, vel inter ipsos patronos, etc., etc. . . . . suspendatur collatio usque ad finem contraversiae, et interim, si opus sit, oeconomum ecclesiae vel beneficio vacanti Ordinarius praeficiat."

APPENDIX

The Jus Patronatus in the United States

The vestiges of the right of patronage in the history of the Church in the United States are so scant as hardly to justify the caption of this appendix. But there are a few references to it in the Acts and Decrees of the Baltimore councils, which testify to the fact it was agitated for in this country, in the earlier days. For, in the year 1829, one finds the first provincial council of Baltimore declaring that: "The jus patronatus and right of appointing and dismissing pastors, claimed by some bodies of trustees, is repugnant to the doctrines and discipline of the Church, and that no right of patronage known to the sacred canons, is vested in any board of trustees or other person or congregation of the laity, or any other individuals in the province; that no collection of money for church purposes has given any right of patronage recognized in canon law."[1]

The second plenary Council (Oct., 1866) bears witness to the fact that up to that time there were many attempts on the part of the laity and of the trustees, especially, to secure for themselves the right of patronage.[2] The words of the Council are the following: "Quoniam graves ortes sunt turbae diversis temporibus in hisce statibus, laicis homiinibus, praesertim aedituis, sibi peoperam assumentibus jus patronatus, Et (Quod magis merandum est) jus institutionis ad ecclesias seu missiones, adeo ut pastores, seu missionarios sibi elegere vellent, etiam invito episcopo, etc., etc., . . . litteris apostolicis sac. mem Pii VIII et Leonis XII, ac S. Congregationis (scil-Propaganda) responsis inhaerentes, hoc nostro decret declaramus, repugnare prorsus doctrinae et disciplinae ecclesiae

1 Acta et Decreta Conc. Prov. Baltimorensis I, No. 6.

2 Acta et Decreta Conc. Plen. Baltimorensis II, Nos. 7-21.

jus illud a laicis assumptum instituendi seu dimittendi pastores: et insuper declaramus nullum jus patronatus cujuscumque generis, quod sacri agnoscant canones, competere nunc alicui personae, laicorum congregationi, aedituorem coetui, seu aliis quibuscumque personis in hac provincia."

After which the Council goes on to give the reasons why the right of patronage was not recognized in the United States, viz., because the required conditions of foundation and endowment (or erection) were not present.

From these quotations—prescinding from their canonical value—it is evident that there are some traces of the right of patronage in the history of the Church in the United States.

The purpose of this discussion is to answer the following questions:

1°—Why was not the Juspatronatus recognized in the United States?

2°—By denying it to our people, was any injustice done them?

3°—Would its admittance have been for the good of the Church here?

The right of patronage was not granted to the Catholic people in the United States for a multitude of reasons.[3] First, it was a privilege of the *common* law of the Church.[4] Since we were a missionary country, and under the jurisdiction of Propaganda, the common law did not apply in our country. Secondly, ever since the Council of Trent,[5] it was the mind of the Church to limit the right of patronage as much as possible. Furthermore, in mission countries (such as the United States was at the time of the councils quoted) *where the common law does not*

3 Hopkin's booklet in Baltimore Diocesan Archives, p. 32-40 (Quoted with permission of Rev. Peter Guilday, Ph.D., of the Catholic University of America, who will soon publish the details of Father Hopkin's booklet).

4 Wernz II, 411-412.

5 Conc. Trid. Sess. XIV, *de ref*, c. 12; Sess. XXV, *de ref*, c. 9. Cf. Wernz II, 415.

obtain, and where benefices in a strict sense do not exist, great freedom is necessary in the election and removal of priests, and hence the right of patronage is ordinarily not admitted.[6] Wherefore, in the collection of the Propaganda of the Faith, there is but *very rare mention* of the juspatronatus—perhaps only two references to it in the whole collection.[7]

But over and above these reasons there is another of far greater moment, which in itself explains the refusal of the juspatronatus among us. It is that voiced in the II Plenary Council of Baltimore, viz., that there was no permanent and certain dowry given to the churches erected in the United States—a necessary condition of the acquisition of the right of patronage, according to the law of the Decretals[8] and Trent.[9] Besides this, the consent of the Ordinary was consistently refused. Also, the subjects who wished the patronal right, viz., the trustees, for the most part, were certainly indisposed to receive any favors from the Church whose constitution they had so frequently violated.[10]

Finally, the manner in which our churches and benefices were founded and erected, did not lend itself to the acquisition of the patronal right. For the Church did not admit the right of patronage to cases where the benefice was erected by means of voluntary offerings of a multitude of the faithful.[11] If she had the result would be that no benefice would be of free collation of the Ordinary, and the monarchial character of the Church would be impugned.

In refusing the right of patronage in the United States, the Church was guilty of no injustice, for the jus-

6 Wernz II, 411; Archiv. 53-229.

7 Cf. Wernz II, p. 173, footnote 50.

8 C. 25, X, de jure patronatus III, 38; cf. Wernz II, 414.

9 Sess. XXV, *de ref*, c. 9; cf. Wernz II, 414.

10 Hopkin's booklet in Baltimore Diocesan Archives.

11 "Quod si ecclesia constructa fuerit ex eleemosynis tantum et devotione populi libera est, non vero de jurepatronatus." S. Cong. Conc. in Cusetina Cappella 19 Nov., 1729, cf. Pallotini XI, 114, par. 45.

patronatus is at most a *jus quaesitum* which can validly be revoked and abolished, even without cause, by the Roman Pontiff.[12] Although, according to Trent (Sess. XXV de ref c 9), it is not equitable to violate the pious wills of the faithful, there is no *injustice* in refusing the right of patronage. It is not even inequitable, where there are good reasons for the refusal as there were in the United States.[13]

As to the probable good which might have been effected by the admittance of the juspatronatus among us, a doubtful response must be given. Judging in retrospect, the good would not have compensated the probable evils to which it could have given rise.[14] The material progress—here we are concerned only with the *material* progress—of the Church in the United States has been second to none in Catholic history. The progress has been made without the help of the juspatronatus; therefore, the probable good which it may have accomplished is very doubtful. Anticipatively, the Church did not admit the juspatronatus in the United States. In view of her proverbial sagacity, therefore, one must conclude that she did not think its admission for the common good of the Church in this country. If one considers the interminable series of abuses to which the right of patronage gave rise throughout the fourteen centuries of its existence, the wisdom of denying the juspatronatus will appear doubly wise.

In conclusion, it is against the spirit of American charity to give with strings attached to offerings. The word of the Lord, "Let not your left hand know what your right had doth," is the motive which actuates American charity. Be that said to the glory of the Church in America.

12 Ferraris v. *juspatronatus* art. IV, 64-66.

13 Ferraris v. juspatronatus art. IV, 64-66; Hopkin's booklet in Baltimore Diocesan Archives.

14 Cf. Statistics of Church in the United States in Bishop England's time (1820-1842) in the "Works of the Rt. Rev. John England," by Reynolds, vol. —, p. —, with the statistics in the Catholic Directory of 1924.

BIBLIOGRAPHY

Sources

The decrees cited in the dissertation will be found among the following works:

Codex Juris Canonici, Romae, 1917.

Acta Apostolicae Sedis, Rome, 1909-1924.

Acta Sanctae Sedis, Rome, 1865-1908.

Codicis Juris Canonici Fontes, Vol. I, Rome, 1923.

Raccolta di Concordati, Rome, 1919.

Canones et Decreta Concilii Tridentini, Rome, 1904.

Acta et Decreta Concilii Plenarii Baltimorensis, II, Baltimore, 1868.

Acta et Decreta Concilii Plenarii Baltimorensis, III, Baltimore, 1886.

Collectanea in usum S. Cong. Epis. et Reg (Bizzari), Rome, 1885.

Corpus Juris Civilis, Krueger-Mommsen, Berlin, 1895.

Bibliography

Archiv fuer Katholisches Kirchenrecht, Innsbruck, 1856-1924.

Catholic Encyclopedia (quoted by title of article), New York, 1907.

Il Monitore Ecclesiastico, Rome 1923-1924.

Herder's Kirchenlexikon, Freiburg in Breisgau, 1895.

Aichner, Dr. Simon, *Compendium Juris Ecclesiastici*, Brescia, 1900.

Augustine, Rev. Chas., *A Commentary on Canon Law*, St. Louis, 1918-1923.

Blat, Fr. Albertus, *Commentarium Textus Codicis Juris Canonici*, Rome, 1921-1923.

Chelodi, Joannes, *Jus Poenale*, Trent, 1920.

Cocchi, Guidus, *Commentarium in Codicem Juris Canonici*, Turin, 1922.

D'Annibale, Jos., *Summula Theologiae Moralis*, Rome, 1892.

Eichmann, *Das Strafgesetz des "Codex Juris Canonici,"* Paderborn, 1920.

Fargna, Francis de, *Commentarium in Canones de Jurepatronatus*, Montisfalisti, 1722.

Ferraris, *Prompta Bibliotheca, etc.*, Paris, 1865.

Hergenroether, *The Catholic Church and Christian State*, London, 1876.

Hinschius, Dr. Paul, *System des Katholischen Kirchenrechts*, Berlin, 1883.

Imbart de la Tour, *Les Paroisses Rurales*, Paris, 1900.

Labbe and Cossart, *Sacrosancta Concilia ad regiam editionem exacta*, 1671-1672.

Mansi, *Sacrorum conciliorum nova et amplissima collectio*, Venice, 1739.

Maroto, *Institutiones Juris Canonici*, Rome, 1921.

Morey, *Outlines of Roman Law*, New York, 1913.

Muratori, A., *Antiquitates italicae medii aevi seu dissertationes*, Milan, 1738-1742.

Philipps, *Kirchenrecht*.

Pirhing, R. P. Enricus, *Jus Canonicum*, Dilingae, 1722.

Reiffenstuel, *Jus Canonicum Universum*, Venice, 1735.

Rossi, Jos., *De Paroecia*, Rome, 1923.

Saegmueller, J. B. *Handbuch des Katholischen Kirchenrechts*, Freiburg in Breisgau, 1900.

Schmalzgrueber, *Jus Ecclesiasticum Universum*, Rome, 1844.

Stutz, U., *Der Geist des Codex Juris Canonici*, Stuttgart, 1918.

Sole, Jacobus, *De Delictis et Poenis*, Rome, 1920.

Thomas, Dr. Paul, *Le Droit de Propriété des Laiques*, Paris, 1906.

Thomassinus, *Vetus et Nova Ecclesiae Disciplina*, Magontiaci, 1787.

Vermeersch, *Epitome Juris Canonici* (Vermeersch-Creusen), Brussels, 1922.

Wernz, F. X., *Jus Decretalium*, Prati, 1915.

(In the dissertation the above works are quoted by the name of the author only.)

DEUS LUX MEA

THESES

quas

AD DOCTORATUS GRADUM

in

JURE CANONICO

APUD UNIVERSITATEM CATHOLICAM AMERICAE

CONSEQUENDUM

PUBLICE PROPUGNABIT

JOANNES ALOISIUS GODFREY, J. C. L.

Sacerdos Archidiocesis Philadelphiensis

Hora 11 A. M.—1 P. M. Die 26 Maii A. D. MCMXXIV

CANONES

I.	Canones	1-7.	De codicis ambitu.
II.	"	17-19.	De legum interpretatione.
III.	"	25-30.	De consuetudinine.
IV.	"	31-35.	De supputatione temporis.
V.	"	49-51.	De rescriptorum interpretatione.
VI.	"	67-69.	De privilegiorum interpretatione.
VII.	"	80-86.	De dispensationibus.
VIII.	"	87-89.	De personis.
IX.	"	96-97.	De consanguinitate et affinitate.
X.	"	99-102.	De personis moralibus.
XI.	"	127-128.	De clericorum obedientia.
XII.	"	147-151.	De provisione canonica.
XIII.	Canon	250.	De S. Congregatione Concilii.
XIV.	"	466.	De Missa pro populo.
XV.	Canones	727-730.	De simonia.
XVI.	"	738-744.	De baptismi ministro.
XVII.	"	1006-1009.	De loco et tempore S. Ordinationis.
XVIII.	"	1035-1042.	De impedimentis in genere.
XIX.	"	1059 & 1080.	De impedimento cognationis legalis.
XX.	Canon	1068.	De impedimento impotentiae.
XXI.	"	1070.	De impedimento disparitatis.

XXII.	Canones	1120-1127.	De privilegio paulino.
XXIII.	"	1205-1210.	De coemeteriis.
XXIV.	"	1250-1254.	De abstinentia et jejunio.
XXV.	"	1337-1348.	De sacris concionibus.
XXVI.	"	1436-1437.	De provisione beneficiorum.
XXVII.	"	1448-1449.	De jure patronatus.
XXVIII.	Canon	1469.	De patronorum oneribus.
XXIX.	"	1471.	De patronatu regio.
XXX.	Canones	1552-1555.	De judiciis in genere.
XXXI.	Canon	1560.	De foro necessario.
XXXII.	Canones	1598-1601.	De S. Romana Rota.
XXXIII.	"	1690-1692.	De mutuis petitionibus.
XXXIV.	"	1701-1705.	De extinctione actionum.
XXXV.	"	1711-1719.	De citatione.
XXXVI.	"	1732-1741.	De litis instantia.
XXXVII.	"	1767-1769.	De jurejurando testium.
XXXVIII.	"	1825-1828.	De praesumptionibus.
XXXIX.	"	2195-2198.	De delictis in genere.
XL.	"	2393-2394.	De delictis in praesentatione.

Jus Publicum Ecclesiasticum:

XLI. De natura sociali Ecclesiae.

XLII. De competentia Ecclesiae in rebus spiritualibus adnexis.

XLIII. De collatione officiorum ecclesiasticorum.

XLIV. De jure quo individua Ecclesiae subjecta bona temporalia possident.

XLV. De Episcopi jurisdictione mediata.

XLVI. De jure Ecclesiae censurandi libros.

XLVII. De praeeminentia Ecclesiae supra Statum.

XLVIII. De jure concordatum.

XLIX. De jure gladii.

L. De ratione conciliorum oecumenicorum.

International Law:

LI. The nature of International Law.

LII. Fundamental principles of International Law.

LIII. The Monroe Doctrine is not based on International Law.

LIV. International law and diplomatic service—their mutual relations.

LV. Concordats must be strictly observed according to the principles of International Law.

LVI. Failure on the part of a nation to pay debts contracted with individuals—whether private or corporate persons—is not sufficient grounds for the declaration of war by the nation whose subjects those individuals are.

LVII. All states have concurrent jurisdiction over pirates.

LVIII. Extradition is legitimate according to the principles of International Law.

LIX. A merchant-vessel is immune from the local jurisdiction of the place where it is stopping.

LX. International Law cannot define the relations between Church and State.

www.ingramcontent.com/pod-product-compliance
Lightning Source LLC
LaVergne TN
LVHW050217080826
844660LV00012B/424

* 9 7 8 0 8 1 3 2 2 2 1 2 7 *